To
Jo,

Be Blessed Shugo !

Tribulation
Or Raptured

Dr [signature]

Tribulation
Or Raptured

The choice is yours!

DR. THOMAS R. SNYDER

Library of Congress Control Number: 2011908501
ISBN: Hardcover   978-1-4628-7846-8
               Softcover   978-1-4628-7845-1
               Ebook   978-1-4628-7847-5
               Audio Book   978-1-4628-8964-8

This book was printed in the United States of America.

All Scripture quotations are taken from *The King James Bible*.

To order additional copies of this book, contact:
Xlibris Corporation
1-888-795-4274
www.Xlibris.com
Orders@Xlibris.com
100116

TESTIMONIES

TABLE OF CONTENTS

DEDICATION

"For God so loved the world!"

This book is dedicated to:
God my Father.
Jesus my Lord and Savior.
The Holy Ghost my Witness.

Also to my loving wife Linda. Who has certainly emulated the character of our Lord Jesus throughout the years. Her continuous encouragement and loyal support, in the writing of this book, has been 'my gift from heaven!'

ACKNOWLEDGEMENTS

I want to personally thank the most precious 'THINK TANK,' who single-handedly applied their expertise to help put this book together and make it work. Your advice and encouraging words will always be part of my heart. Also, all my brothers and sisters at Lamb of God for your faithfulness, prayers, fastings and love for our Lord Jesus throughout the writing of this book. You have all helped me to fill a vital part of my call in the earth. My heartfelt thanks.

FOREWORD

I've known Dr. Thomas R Snyder for some years. A graduate of the 'Jesus Calls Institute of Power Ministry,' August 12, 1988. Over the years, he has certainly demonstrated the power of the Holy Ghost working through him, with signs and wonders, especially the gifts of healing.

His gifted ability to write in the Holy Spirit, gives this book a simplistic design, nevertheless, speaks volumes of revelation.

As the reader, your heart will melt with the warmth of God's presence, as the testimonies unfold the matchless love of God. A treasure chest of literary genius as only God can give.

Dr. Snyder is always prompt to magnify the name of Jesus, giving all the glory to God!

"He is known to me as a man who lives by what he preaches and reflects the presence of Christ thru his life."

Dr. Paul Dhinakaran
Jesus Calls Ministries

PREFACE

Like a carbon copy over laid on the creator's master plan, this world we are living in is repeating what once happened in Noah's flood. All of the ingredients are present. Even the word of God proclaims that this world is ready to give birth once again to God's sovereign intervention. Learn as this blueprint of facts unfolds, chapter by chapter, revealing an insight into the scriptures as few have ever shared, that will be yours.

Did Methuselah, Noah's grandfather, perish with the flood? What does this mean to us today? Is God's history repeating itself and can we avoid the mistakes Methuselah made?

The great and mighty masterpiece of all is the glorious plan of the rapture. Through this event, Father God, makes an escape route for his people; while quarantining the devil, leaving him no escape route. Through the rapture, our Lord has devised a way to bring his banished home to himself, without having to experience death or corruption. It is the only future event, in the heart of God, that can come at any time, as a thief in the night.

It is impossible for the child of light to miss the rapture or not know when it will take place. You will explore in depth this immutable truth, that the children of light will not be caught as a thief in the night. Learn how you too can be guaranteed not to miss the rapture.

There isn't a person alive that hasn't looked up to the heavens, enveloped in their awesome existence, and not have had thoughts about eternity. Truly in the heart of man, there has been placed a desire to know what awaits them after leaving this earth. This is why when a miracle is witnessed or read about it unlocks these areas of mysteries with divine reassurance. This divine reassurance confirms that there is a God and he does communicate with man. Like a brush in an artist's hand, the scriptures will paint a perfect picture of clarity of what awaits us in heaven.

Jesus' appearance in heaven reveals that he is wearing many crowns. Everyone will receive a crown on that day of judgment, a reflective of Almighty God rewarding according to their deeds. Even the disobedient shall receive a crown. Yes, that's right, people that will go to hell receive a crown! There are six crowns that you and I are eligible for. Each one will be examined thoroughly for their attributes.

All over the world, the body of Christ is crying out to Almighty God, their heavenly Father, for more of the Holy Ghost. Iniquity is abounding and there is a stir in the hearts of all Saints. Could this be the forerunner of the latter rain? In order to grasp the importance of the times we are in, we must first establish whether God has ordained a latter rain: a second Pentecost. So unshakable is the word of God, rich with wisdom and knowledge, that we only need to reach out with our faith to be filled to satisfaction.

After the rapture takes place, the scene on the earth will be drastically altered. Now instead of the Dragon, alias Lucifer, Satan, devil and the serpent, persecuting the Saints, Almighty God begins to pour out his wrath on the Dragon and all the inhabitants of the earth. This is the beginning of the great tribulation. Each and every detail of this event will be truly revealed along with a timetable concerning future events. *You do not want to go through this great tribulation.* Learned how to avoid this experience.

Throughout the Bible, 'the architect of our soul' has designed examples of people and personalities to learn from. Many will come to life in this publication, emulating God's infinite wisdom.

There is a holy boldness that will accompany the true believer. Without debate, every time God worked his divine will on this earth, he chose holy boldness to be the main ingredient. In order to attain this main ingredient you must have the Holy Ghost.

Many people today are worried about the end of the world, the rapture, the tribulation, the Antichrist, the economy or just the future in general concerning this world in which we live. There is only one antidote to resolve this weariness of mind. In chapter 8 of this publication, you will find that remedy.

Volumes have been written concerning the Antichrist, the number '666', and the events surrounding the tribulation. Jesus himself gives us some very encouraging enlightenment concerning this entire subject. Learn about the lukewarm church and how to identify it and where the true church is in these end times.

Flavored into each chapter you will read of wondrous and marvelous miracles that Jesus has performed through Dr. Snyder. You will be in awe, as the recipients of Almighty God's grace and power reveal their heartfelt testimonies. Chapter one awaits!

CHAPTER 1

Enoch:
The First Rapture

Like a carbon copy over laid on the Creator's Master Plan, this world we are living in is repeating what once happened in Noah's flood. All of the ingredients are present; a falling away from the love of the truth, iniquity is abounding, and so on. Even the word of God proclaims that this world is ready to give birth once again to God's sovereign intervention. As the blueprint unfolds, we must begin at the beginning with the first forerunner of the rapture, Enoch.

Enoch is the first pioneer in religion. A dedicated disciple through which God, demonstrates his abilities to transfigure or "rapture" a person from one world into another, **'while they are still alive!'** Enoch's inception is found in Genesis 5:18-24.

In order to understand who Enoch is and how he relates to the coming rapture, the lukewarm church, and his son Methuselah, we have to first start at the beginning with creation itself. When God created Adam and Eve and walked among them, HE never speaks anything in his creation concerning leaving this earth and living with HIM elsewhere. As commonly expressed today, "Are you going to heaven when you die?" As of yet, there was no expression from our creator, in the earth, concerning another place that man could attain; where God himself lives. The intent was that man would be obedient to all of God's commandments, eat of the tree of life, and live forever on this earth. However, we realize that this did not happen, and death has become evident to everyone of us. In Psalms 115:16, the Bible tells us that the heavens are the Lord's and HE has given the earth to man. *The heaven, even the heavens, are the Lord's: but the earth hath he given to the children of men* (Psalm 115:16). In the first chapters of Genesis, creation took place in six days and on the seventh day God rested. Enoch is the seventh generation from Adam, expressing hope to all mankind. What is this hope? *And Enoch walked with God: and he was not; for God took him* (Genesis 5:24). Again in Hebrews 11:5 it says *"By faith Enoch was translated that he should not see death."* **YES, HE WAS RAPTURED!!** This confirming that the creator's desire has not changed. HIS desires are to spend eternity with created man. Just like Father God entered into HIS rest; **REST IN THAT FACT!**

I received a prayer request concerning the deliverance of someone who was unstable of mind. She was in an institution and the person making the request was the nurse attending to her. She had heard that Jesus was doing the miraculous through this man of God. As I prayed over the telephone, Jesus instructed me to tell her that the devil had to go out of her mind. That he himself would personally visit her and a miracle would take place. However, the very night of the prayer this person jumped up out of bed, went out the window and ran barefoot through the snow to get away. The devil is a rascal, and he will do all he can to stop the mercies and love that God has for all mankind. The person who made the prayer request called me the next day and related what had happened. The Holy Spirit said to tell her "what God has said, He has said." I then reassured her that the miracle would take place; that Jesus would visit and God would be glorified. Because of this event the patient was discharged and found herself living with her niece. Here is the testimony of what happened next, in her own words:

Thank you for praying for Mrs. B. She is living with her niece now, since that night she went out of the window in the freezing weather.

When she first moved in, she was still trying to get out. She was up all night beating on the door and conversing with her deceased sister, husband and grandmother. She said, "they were ready to go and she had to leave." The niece locked the door from the outside that night by using nails and chords. After contacting her doctor, the next night, she safe proofed the room by installing a deadbolt lock on the door, to be opened only with a key. Well, Dr. Snyder, things were looking grim. I encouraged her to believe God because 'the man of God' had told me that the devil had to go, and it would be rough for a while, but she will be free in Jesus' name. She agreed. Then, she and her husband anointed their houseguest with oil and prayed, reminding the Lord of your words that HE had spoken through you. Later, in the week, she was put down for a noon nap. She awakened with a prayer and came out of her room with a different appearance. She said, "a fog like a cloud came over her in bed." When it went away, she felt like a new person and her mind is so much clearer. She even remembered a secret and special account her late husband had left her. She remembered the bank and everything! The niece being reluctant, encouraged her to call the bank for herself and sure enough it was true.

A fog like cloud came over her! In Exodus 19:9, we can read, '*lo I come unto thee in a thick cloud.*' In Exodus 19:16, '*a thick cloud came upon the mountain.*' In Numbers 9:16, '*and a cloud covered the Tabernacle by day.*' In Exodus 14:19, '*and the pillar of the cloud went with the Israelites.*' In 2

Chronicles 5:13, '*and the house of God was filled with a cloud.*' In Matthew 17:5, '*and a bright cloud overshadowed them on the Mount of Transfiguration.*' In Acts 1:9, '*and a cloud received Jesus out of their sight.*'

Then in Acts 1:11 it says, '*he shall return in like manner.*' Jesus truly is *the same yesterday, today and forever* (Hebrews 13:8). So you see, Jesus did come and personally visit with her; **HE CAME IN A CLOUD!** Jesus prophesied of the rapture in Luke 17:34. *I tell you, in that night there shall be two men in one bed; the one shall be taken, and the other shall be left* (Luke 17:34). In the chapter titled, 'Raptured! In the Twinkle of the Eye,' we will explore this future event in detail. In the book of Revelation 14:14, through the awesome wisdom and power of God, Jesus will come in a cloud and personally perform the miracle of the rapture.

Until Enoch's rapture, there was no manifested expression of God's eternal purpose towards mankind. There were no Ten Commandments, no temple, no Jesus; only the continual living of the curses. The curses were death and that of the ground being cursed. Father God gave promise of a Messiah. However, he was a promise not a manifestation as of yet. When Enoch is born to Jared, this starts the supernatural communication with man concerning Father God's first expression of eternal life. He desires us to live with him eternally in a place other than earth (Heaven, Paradise, the kingdom of God). We know that there will be a new heaven and the new earth, although it has not been manifested as of this present time. *Nevertheless, we, according to his promise, look for new heavens and a new earth, wherein dwelleth righteousness* (2 Peter 3:13).

When God said of Enoch that he should not see death, we can clearly see the mercies of God being expressed concerning the first curse "death." In the chapter titled 'Noah' Master Builder! we will encounter Almighty God's unfailing mercies towards the second curse.

Enoch was 65 years old when he birthed his first child, a son, naming him Methuselah. It's interesting to see that Enoch first started 'walking with God' after the birth of his son. Methuselah will be a key personality in this publication. As these pages unfold, we will discover that although 'Enoch was his father and Noah his grandson, he 'missed the boat' and perished with the flood.' Methuselah represents the present-day lukewarm church, **THAT WILL MISS THE RAPTURE!** Why do I say this? Let's take a closer look at the character of Methuselah's father, Enoch. In the book of Jude, starting in verse 14, we read, *And Enoch also, the seventh from Adam, prophesied of these, saying, Behold, the Lord cometh with ten thousand of his saints, to execute judgment upon all, and to convince all that are ungodly among them of all their ungodly deeds which they have ungodly committed and of all their hard speeches which ungodly sinners have spoken against him. These are murmurs, complainers, walking after their own lusts; and their mouth speaketh great swelling words having men's persons in admiration because of advantage* (Jude 14-16).

Methuselah lived with his father Enoch three hundred years before God raptured him, and he was not; Hebrews 11:5. Do you think, after surveying the character of his father Enoch, that Methuselah heard similar words from his father's mouth on a daily basis? Not only is it recorded that Enoch walked with God, but also that he pleased him; Hebrews 11:5. After experiencing his father's rapture, one might have thought a tremendous overwhelming impact would have occurred in his life. Methuselah knew that he would have to face death and deal with the same God who was so very close to his father. That this God, whom his father Enoch served with all his heart, had power over life and death. Nevertheless, nothing, no nothing, is recorded in the Bible about Methuselah's spiritual life or relationship with God.

When Methuselah is 187 years old he birthed his first child, a son, naming him Lamech. Lamech will continue to carry the torch of God's unfailing love to the human race. What was his message that had such a paramount effect on the whole world and should it be heeded today?

CHAPTER 2

Lamech
Prophet of God

Throughout the Bible 'the architect of our soul' has designed examples of people and personalities to learn from. Lamech is one of them. Not only was he a prophet of God, but he was the only recorded prophet of God to the first world. That's right! The only one. No one else before the flood spoke of any future event besides God himself. So what was his prophecy? What was his word to the whole human race?

In Genesis chapter 5:29, we read this, *And he (Lamech) called his name Noah, saying, This same shall comfort us concerning our work and toil of our hands, because of the ground which the Lord hath cursed.* Most remarkable that at the birth of his first child, Noah, Lamech would have knowledge of an event that would take place six hundred years in the future. Is this possible, that someone could see the future under the power of God's Spirit? This is what is called prophecy. Words of comfort and exultation, concerning future events. Here is a testimony I received, confirming God's abilities to speak through man.

I received a telephone call one afternoon concerning someone who was in labor with child. She had all of her children at home. Complications arose and she was bleeding. Here is what happened in her own words:

We have our children at home and during the early stages of labor only a girlfriend was present. The midwife had not yet arrived. As labor progressed a complication occurred and I asked my friend to call Dr. Thomas R Snyder for prayer. He called back about fifteen to twenty minutes later. He shared a vision with me that the Lord had given him, as he interceded for me. In the vision he said,

"I was hanging out diapers on a clothes line. Turning to him, I exclaimed, 'I have seen the power of the Lord." Furthermore, he added, " that no matter what happens; don't go by sight, that **the baby would live!"** The phone call from this 'man of God' quieted my spirit and I began to rest in the Lord's peace.

When our daughter was born, she gave out one cry and then was very quiet and still. The midwife checked for a heartbeat and pulse, but found none. C.P.R. was started on her tiny body, but she did not respond. An incredible peace filled the room. I knew it was the Lord's presence. Minutes ticked by and still she did not respond to the C.P.R. Then, I remembered the vision Dr. Snyder had shared with me. I thought in my heart if he truly is 'a man of God,' the baby would live. I would see the power of God giving back life. I cried out to the Lord from the very depths of my soul for her life. I heard the midwife say, "I've got a pulse!" Our baby was alive!

I praise Jesus for his tender mercy and love toward us that night. I am forever grateful to him for raising up servants who allow the gifts to work in their lives; such as he has done with Dr. Snyder. We truly had seen the 'power of the Lord.' **The vision became fact!**

This was a future event that hadn't happened. When this event occurred, life and death would be in the balance. God chooses to be merciful and compassionate, by telling us ahead of time what he's able to do concerning these events, if we only believe! Lamech had Almighty God's mind on a future event that would affect each and every person in the whole earth. But what went wrong? What happened that even Lamech's own father, Methuselah, missed the boat on the whole matter? Is this also a message for today?

In second Chronicles 20:20, God has laid down this foundation of fact: *Believe in the Lord your God, so shall ye be established; believe his prophets so shall ye prosper.* In the testimony we have just shared, the mother had to believe what the prophet said and call on the name of Jesus in her time of trouble. *I will take the cup of salvation, and call upon the name of the Lord* (Psalms 116:13). Calling on God and having faith in God are very close sisters. I'm sure that when Lamech's prophecy concerning his son, Noah, began to unfold through his construction of the ark, people began to wonder. Perhaps thoughts of "could it all be true?" filled many minds. After all, here is a rather large boat being built on dry land in the middle of nowhere. Where would the water come from? Up until now, the earth was being watered only from beneath. *But there went up a mist from the earth, and watered the whole face of the ground* (Genesis 2:6). Just as many people are wondering today; "**where is this world going?**" I'm persuaded that when the prophecy was fulfilled and the flood began to occur, there were a lot of people calling on God. But it was too late! The prophet had spoken, it's reality was all around; no one on the whole face of the earth, at that time, believed him. Otherwise, God would have made room for them on the ark and included them in his work. Why his work also? *Even so faith, if it hath not works, is dead, being alone* (James 2: 17).

Lamech seems to be a reflection of the true church today, continually reinforcing the true word of God, giving revelation, authority and power to the greatness of Jesus' name.

So, what was taking place on the earth at that time? According to Luke 17:26-28, they were eating and drinking. They married wives and were giving themselves in marriage until Noah went into the ark. Also, it refers to the days of Lot as being the same as the days of Noah; they did eat, they drank, they bought, they sold, they planted, they built. Need I say more? Yes, peace and prosperity seem to be the echoes of the past in this present day lukewarm church age; supposing that gain is godliness. *Perverse disputings of men of corrupt minds, and destitute of the truth, supposing that gain is godliness: from such withdraw thyself* (1 Timothy 6:5).

The Lord Jesus said that he would prepare the church, the body of Christ, so that it would appear pure before God. *That he might present it to himself a glorious church, not having spot, or wrinkle, or any such thing; but that it should be holy and without blemish* (Ephesians 5:27). As Jesus prepares a place for you, *And if I go and prepare a place for you, I will come again, and receive you unto myself; that where I am, there ye may be also* (John 14:3). We are advised, in Ephesians 2:20, to prepare an habitable place for God, through the Spirit. We will read in the chapter titled 'The Lukewarm Church,' how to clearly see the difference, between lukewarm and being on fire for God!

When the word of Noah's prophecy was being fulfilled and Noah's relationship with God grew stronger, mankind seemed to be completely uninterested. There was a one hundred year span from when God spoke to Noah and when the ark was completed. You and I know that people will talk. How merciful God was to let the message go out into all the known world for one hundred years. I cannot imagine what they were thinking. All the evidence points to this conclusion, they frankly did not believe Lamech's prophecy. Perhaps, the world did not understand; being ignorant of God's methods or how He would remove the curse. Even today, there are some people experiencing these same elements. Chapter twelve of this book titled, 'Raptured! In the Twinkle of the Eye,' will detail man's future.

Jesus, while on earth, talked about two specific coming events, amongst others. The first event is the rapture. *I tell you, in that night there shall be two men in one bed; the one shall be taken and the other shall be left. Two women shall be grinding together; the one shall be taken, the other left* (Luke17: 34 & 35). Confirming the same in 1 Thessalonians. *Then we which are alive and remain shall be caught up together with them in the clouds, to meet the Lord in the air: and so shall we ever be with the Lord* (1 Thessalonians 4:17). The second event Jesus talked about is the end of time, or better put, *the end of this world*, which can be found in the gospel of Matthew. *So shall it be at the end of the world: the angels shall come forth, and sever the wicked from among the just* (Matthew 13:49). Confirming the same in 2 Peter: *But the day of the Lord will come as a thief in the night; in the which the heavens shall pass away with a great noise, and the elements shall melt with fervent heat, the earth also and the works that are therein shall be burned up* (2 Peter 3:10). There are also many other references in the Bible concerning these two extraordinary events. They will not be altered; **what God has said, he has said!**

So many people are under strong delusion that these events will not happen. We can see that the scenery in the world is changing, setting the stage for such events. Many are acting exactly as they did in Noah's time. Yes! Noah's time. 'History repeating itself' seems to have a familiar ring. Just look around. Could what happened to the people in Noah's world be happening today? In the next chapter titled, 'Noah' Master Builder! the mist shall rise and we will find the answer.

CHAPTER 3

'Noah'
Master Builder!

The second curse brought in by Adam and Eve was the curse of the ground. *And unto Adam he said, Because thou hast hearkened unto the voice of thy wife, and hast eaten of the tree, of which I commanded thee, saying, Thou shalt not eat of it: cursed is the ground for thy sake; in sorrow shalt thou eat of it all the days of thy life* (Genesis 3:17). In order to remove this curse, God needed a master builder. Why a master builder? Noah not only would build the ark, but also establish a spiritual covenant with God concerning the ground and mankind. This agreement was so binding that it still continues today and will unto the end of time.

As we look at what took place in 'Noah's flood,' it may seem cruel to us that God only saved Noah and his family. However, no one else wanted to be saved, at least not on God's terms. Putting it another way, all fell short of the requirements of righteousness. *And God saw that the wickedness of man was great in the earth, and that every imagination of the thoughts of his heart was only evil continually* (Genesis 6:5). *But Noah found grace in the eyes of the Lord* (Genesis 6:8). One may say that grace is not righteousness, but I disagree. *That as sin hath reigned unto death, even so might grace reign through righteousness unto eternal life by Jesus Christ our Lord* (Romans 5:21). If Noah found grace in the eyes of the Lord, it was available to all.

God was willing to help everyone who was alive at that time. It seemed that no one took God seriously concerning an event they knew very little about. Being ignorant of the fact or having a shallow understanding of what was about to take place, will harbor no excuses. Righteousness is always a pre-requisite of being saved. Jesus, through the blood of his living sacrifice, is our righteousness! *Whom God hath set forth to be a propitiation through faith in his blood, to declare his righteousness for the remission of sins that are past, through the forbearance of God* (Romans 3:25).

During this one hundred year span, when Noah and his family were building the ark, fulfilling the prophecy that his father Lamech gave, people were receiving a "birds eye view" of that fact. Not even his own grandfather Methuselah took it seriously. If he had, something would have been attributed to his name concerning involvement with God's business or his hearing from God. How could these things be? Did this loving, gracious and good God, who created everything, including man, forget himself? As God surveyed the success of his creation on the sixth day, he concludes "it is very good!" *And God saw everything that he had made, and, behold, it was very good. And the evening and the morning were the sixth day* (Genesis 1:31). In the book of Isaiah, we read that our ways and thoughts are not God's ways or thoughts. *For my thoughts are not your thoughts, neither are your ways my ways, saith the Lord* (Isaiah 55:8).

As we take a closer look at what took place and who was saved from the first world, we find that everything Almighty God took in quantity was pure, clean, and righteous unto Him. God is not a destroyer of goodness.

He hates evildoers. *I have hated the congregation of evildoers; and will not sit with the wicked* (Psalms 26:5). God even goes as far as to say, *And it repented the Lord that he made man on the earth, and it grieved him at his heart* (Genesis 6:6). Nothing, no nothing was lost that truly wanted to please God, to keep his ways, or was rescued through God's anointed, Noah. Just like Jesus, God's only begotten son, redeems and prepares us today for the events that are coming.

The facts were all around them just as they are today! No one seemed to know how God was going to redeem the curse of the ground. All of this was new to them. Unlike the first world, we have a witness! Just what is that witness?

I received a telephone call from someone in North Carolina. They were diagnosed with cancer and had a smoking habit for over forty years. She was seeking healing from Jesus, but had doubts in her heart. This is the testimony she gave in her own words.

> I was very sick. Thinking I had pneumonia, I went to the doctor. X-rays showed I had spots on one lung and I was told to quit smoking. Given cough medicine and some pills for anxiety; I was also told to see a specialist concerning my lung. Upon seeing the specialist, it was concluded the spots were cancer and immediate removal of part of my lung was necessary to prolong life. Surgery was immediately set up for that Monday.

> That Friday before going to the hospital, I called Dr. Thomas R Snyder and asked if Jesus could heal me? I had doubts in my heart. I felt unworthy to receive such a powerful healing from God. Dr. Snyder explained, under the anointing of the Holy Spirit, God's mercies, truth, compassion and love Jesus had for all that turned to him in need of such miracles in their life. He then, being moved with tears prayed a most powerful prayer over the telephone (as he was in Wisconsin and I was in North Carolina at the time) that my lung would be made whole by the powerful unfailing name of Jesus, and all desire of smoking be removed.

I went into the hospital on that Monday for scheduled surgery. A few more tests were made. All of a sudden, a nurse entered into my hospital room and said, **"the surgery was canceled!"** After asking if she had the right patient, because the x-rays showed that the cancer and the spots where no longer present in the lung. All I could say was thank you Jesus. Thank you Jesus!! I couldn't wait to call Dr. Snyder that afternoon and give him the glorious news of what Jesus had done. How God responded to his compassionate prayer concerning the complete healing of my lung and deliverance from smoking. That's right! At that time, Jesus did a double miracle. After forty years of smoking a carton of cigarettes per week, I haven't had one since. That was almost eleven months ago.

In this testimony, she did not know how a miracle took place. Neither did she know much about God. This she did know, that she needed help, and after listening to what the word of God said, the rest is history.

So, what is the witness that we have today? **THE WORD OF GOD!** Which is the **Bible**. *All scripture is given by inspiration of God, and is profitable for doctrine, for reproof, for correction, for instruction in righteousness* (2 Timothy 3:16). Yes, the word of God proclaims in 1 Thessalonians 4:17, that there will first be a rapture of God's people, both the living and the dead, from this earth. After that, Revelation 20:6 proclaims, a thousand year reign upon this earth, with Jesus Christ himself personally seated in Jerusalem. Then and only then, will the event described in 2 Peter 3:10 take place; the earth will melt with fervent heat. This will be the end of this world! Believe it or not **these events will happen!** Simply because the word of God proclaims them!

Where is God's goodness in all of this? *Nevertheless, we, according to his promise, look for new heavens and a new earth, wherein dwelleth righteousness*

(2 Peter 3:13). However, keep this in mind, that you must be **born again!**; And Jesus answered, *Verily, verily, I say unto thee, Except a man be born of water and of the Spirit, he cannot enter into the kingdom of God* (John 3:5). Without this true conversion of your soul you cannot enter the kingdom of God, John 3:5-8, which will be the new earth and the new heavens. *And I saw a new heaven and a new earth: for the first heaven and the first earth were passed away; and there was no more sea* (Revelation 21:1).

When Noah built the ark, God gave him a blueprint from heaven. In Genesis 6:16, it's interesting to see that in God's master plan, that Noah was instructed to build three levels in the ark. In the book of 2 Corinthians 12:2 the apostle Paul was caught up to the third heaven; reflective of two more levels. I'm persuaded that when 'the books are open' on that great day of the Lord, He will position every believer according to their works, Revelation 20:12. This will be expounded on later in the chapter titled 'The Books Were Opened.'

Equally impressive is that God waited seven days before shutting the door of the ark, Genesis 7:4. Why did he wait seven days? We are made aware of this fact that God was long-suffering in the days of Noah, while the ark was being prepared, 1 Peter 3:20. Just like He is longsuffering today, that none should perish, 2 Peter 3:9. Perhaps, God went to Methuselah and reasoned with him. There is a similar event that took place in the book of Genesis chapter 19. There the Lord, after talking to Abraham concerning Lot and his family, went forth to save them, before destroying everything.

They were in Sodom and Gomorrah and God was prepared to destroy that city, and He did! The character of God is to save and not destroy. However, you must reason with him! *Surely I would speak to the Almighty, and I desire to reason with God* (Job 13:3). Yes, the goodness of the Lord is gracious, long-suffering, slow to anger and plenteous in mercies. God is reasoning with the world today! Whatever your situation is, bring it to Jesus, he will undertake!

The flood has now come and gone. The waters are abated. We now have the New World. Along with Noah, there are three more characters that will begin to shape the future of mankind, Noah's sons: Shem, Ham, and Japheth. This is important because when God speaks of blessings in the New World, He speaks not only to Noah but to his sons also. *And God spake unto Noah, and to his sons with him, saying, And I, behold, I establish my covenant with you, and with your seed after you* (Genesis 9:8–9). It is important for all hearts to be right before God, because one life effects another. Noah's son Ham, after seeing all that his father Noah faithfully went through, how clearly he heard God's voice, and carried out God's plan, seemed to be unmoved by all of this. Ham also experienced the awesome power of God's wrath along with his great mercies but wasn't moved one bit in character. Fully knowing that he would have perished with the flood, along with his great-grandfather Methuselah, had Noah his father not been a chosen vessel. Ham chooses to demonstrate criticism, pride, and arrogance by showing his father Noah's nakedness. *And Ham, the father of Canaan, saw the nakedness of his father, and told his two brethren without* (Genesis 9:22). Ham's nature will now begin to be carried on through the ages, passing down from generation to generation, teaching others these ungodly habits.

The ark had not come to rest for very long in the New World, just long enough for Noah to grow a vineyard. Ham received **'the first curse'** in the New World. *And he said, Cursed be Canaan; a servant of servants shall he be unto his brethren* (Genesis 9:25).

The ark is now resting on dry ground. Noah is commanded by God to go from the ark. Without being told by God, in Genesis 8:20, Noah respectfully builds an altar unto the Lord and offers burnt offerings. *And the Lord smelled a sweet savour; and the Lord said in his heart, I will not again curse the ground any more for man's sake; for the imagination of man's heart is evil from his youth; neither will I again smite anymore every living thing, as I have done* (Genesis 8:21). This covenant is made with Noah and every generation to follow. God goes on further to say, *While the earth remainth, seed time and harvest, and cold and heat, and summer and winter, and day and night shall not cease* (Genesis 8:22). **The curse to the ground has been redeemed!** Our earth will yield her fruit, year after year and season after season, and cannot and will not be altered by man's hand.

God reaffirms His creation formula once again in Genesis 9:1-10. This time, no matter how evil man gets, we have God's promise, that He will never again curse the ground a second time. How great are his mercies! This promise is perpetual for all generations. To confirm this covenant, God set the rainbow in the clouds for a token to the earth. *And the bow shall be in the cloud; and I will look upon it, that I may remember the everlasting covenant between God and every living creature of all flesh that is upon the earth* (Genesis 9:16).

Where is Methuselah in all of this? It is evident, that he was not on the ark. Did he really miss the boat and perished with the flood? The evidence will be found in the next chapter titled, Methuselah 'Prisoner of Time.'

CHAPTER 4

Methuselah
'Prisoner of Time'

Logic dictates that either Methuselah perished in the flood or as a result of the flood! More simply put, there no longer remained an habitable earth that would support life. It no longer had God's favor. Therefore, death was imminent.

Proverbs 25:2 tells us, *It is the glory of God to conceal a thing: but the honour of kings is to search out a matter.* As we search through the fifth chapter of Genesis, we will find that Methuselah is recorded to have died the exact time of the flood. Can you imagine that! After living nine hundred and sixty nine years, having had associations with three mighty men of God, his father Enoch, his son Lamech, and his grandson Noah, that day caught him unawares. The most awesome event in the history of mankind, by the mighty hand of God, took place and caught him completely by surprise. Like a thief in the night so was his demise. Today, too many people are either unaware of or are unknowledgeable concerning what God is doing and about to do in the earth. Let's put the numbers together and see for yourself that Methuselah perished with the flood.

The foundation of facts will be found in Genesis 5:19-32. Finishing up with the sixth verse of Genesis chapter 7. Beginning in Genesis 5: 19, we can read that Enoch is born to Jared. Then, when Enoch is sixty five years old,

Methuselah is birth to him. At the age of three hundred and sixty five years old, Enoch is raptured. Methuselah was one hundred eighty seven years old when he birthed his first son, Lamech. The Scriptures then reveal this gem of fact; Methuselah died at the ripe old age of nine hundred sixty nine years, Genesis 5:7. Most disciples of the Scriptures are content with knowing at what age he died, thinking that exactly where this verse is placed in the Scriptures completes his natural life. Therefore, equipped with this reasoning, it would be impossible for him to be involved with any future Scripture or event and bring closure to the natural life of Methuselah. After all, the natural mind has placed him in the grave in Genesis 5:27. However, according to the date that God has given to us concerning his death, not the placement of the verse, he is alive and well until Genesis 7:6. Here are the dates:

Name	Age	Description
Methuselah	-187 years-	* birth of Lamech (Genesis 5:25)
Methuselah	-782 years-	lived after he birthed Lamech (Genesis 5:26)
Methuselah	-969 years-	age of his death (Genesis 5:27)
	—————	
Lamech	-182 years-	birth of Noah (Genesis 5:28-29)
Methuselah*	(+)-187 years-	age at Lamech's birth *(see above)
	—————	

Methuselah	-369 years-	his age at Noah's birth
Noah	-500 years-	**age of Noah when God speaks to him (Genesis 5:32) .
	_____	
Methuselah-	-869 years-	** age of Methuselah when God spoke to Noah.
Noah	-600 years-	*** age of Noah when the flood waters came upon the earth (Genesis 7:6)
Methuselah	+100 years	from when God spoke to Noah and the flood came.
Methuselah	-969 years-	*** age of Methuselah at time of flood

This is the same age recorded in Genesis 5:27 of Methuselah's death. Either he perished with the flood or as a result of the flood. **You be the judge!!!**

Lamech	-777 years-	his age at his death (Genesis 5:31)
Lamech	(+)187 years	*** to catch up to Methuselah life span
	_____	
Lamech	-964 years-	Methuselah out lived his son Lamech by five years

Lamech died five years before the flood; however, Methuselah died the same year of the flood! There are no coincidences with God. Everything, from the most minute detail, even the unseen, is ordered by His mighty breath and hand.

Why is God revealing this revelation today? Is there a need for enlightenment concerning present-day events? Perhaps this testimony will help.

> Over two years ago, I suffered a stroke which left me completely without a voice. I could not make any vocal sounds at all. In the process of time, (approximately a year later), still enslaved by the same condition, Lamb of God Ministries visited the nursing home in which I am a resident.

> After the program of the gospel of Jesus Christ (in song and word), I could feel the presence of the Lord in our midst. The organist, upon noticing my condition, strongly suggested that Dr. Snyder pray for me; telling me how wonderfully God worked through his prayers and how Jesus did the most wonderful miracles. In response, I motioned that I desired Dr. Snyder to pray for me. As he anointed me with oil in Jesus' name, he laid his hands on my head. I don't remember everything he spoke, but this I do remember my faith started to build and I felt a sensation in my tongue.

> Throughout the year on a few more occasions, Dr. Snyder prayed with tears and power **in Jesus' name!** that the string of my tongue would be loosed. Then it happened, my voice started to return. Without any therapy whatsoever, I can speak clearly, hold a conversation and praise the Lord Jesus with a shout.

Jesus has given me my voice back. I cannot tell you how much this means to me. I was totally dumb until Dr. Snyder brought Jesus' healing power to myself, like no one else could!

After I could speak, Dr. Snyder asked me if I had believed that God worked through people this way? To bring Jesus' divine power and love from God such as healing, deliverance, salvation, and so on. My answer was yes! He seemed surprised. He then asked, "why did I wait so long to find someone to pray with me and receive a miracle?" I answered because, in all my life, no one came along to prayed with me like you, in the character of a true disciple of Jesus Christ. Just professing to know Jesus is not enough, you Dr. Snyder showed me you know him and openly demonstrated this when Jesus heard your prayer and gave me my voice back.

Thanking God wholeheartedly. Giving all the glory, honor and praise to Jesus, who has given of his resurrected power to such servants as Dr. Thomas R Snyder.

Yes, professing to know Jesus is not enough. *They profess that they know God; but in works they deny him* (Titus 1: 16a). Don't end up like Methuselah and miss the signs of the times.

After his death, Methuselah became a 'prisoner of time.' *By which also he (Jesus) went and preached unto the spirits in prison; Which sometime were disobedient, when once the long-suffering of God waited in the days of Noah, while the ark was a preparing, wherein few , that is, eight souls were saved by water*(1 Peter 3: 19-20). Before Jesus rose from the dead, he first went to the spirits that perished in Noah's flood. Methuselah had been a prisoner for *a* long time. The word prisoner is always accompanied by undesirable fellow travelers, concerning one's free will. Equally, today associations with religion only, instead of with Jesus, will cause a missing of the rapture, resulting in a similar fate. *For as a snare shall it come on all them that dwell on the face of the whole earth. Watch ye therefore, and pray always, that ye may be accounted worthy to escape all these things that shall come to pass, and to stand before the Son of man* (Luke 21: 35 & 36). Yes, all that miss the rapture and remain will have to go through the tribulation.

Methuselah chose to remain exactly the way he was. He was content with his daily routine, accepting instead of expecting. In the testimony you have just read, she was willing to hear what the word of God said, trust in the man of God, and allow the Lord to work accordingly. It was shared earlier in this chapter that Methuselah had three pronounced men of God in his life. He also experienced the awesome power of God. Was he just confused? What was blinding him concerning God's reality in and around his life? Methuselah was experiencing what 'the lukewarm church' is experiencing today. In our next chapter, titled the same, the search for answers will thoroughly be furnished.

CHAPTER 5

The Lukewarm Church

The lukewarm church is commonly referred to as the 'end of times church' and can be found in the book of Revelation. *Because thou sayest, I am rich, and increased with goods, and have need of nothing; and knowest not that thou art wretched, and miserable, and poor, and blind, and naked* (Revelation 3:17). Wealthy, in need of nothing, yet poor. Displaying a form of godliness, but denying the power of God. *Having a form of godliness but denying the power thereof: from such turn away* (2 Timothy 3:5). Methuselah, in the days of Noah, his grandson, was buying and selling, giving in marriage, building and so on (all the elements of this world). Both the lukewarm church and Methuselah were calling their lifestyle "the will of God."

When Jesus was on the earth, he started no social entertainment programs. He instituted the power of God to meeting men's needs. *How God anointed Jesus of Nazareth with the Holy Ghost and with power: who went about doing good, and healing all that were oppressed of the devil; for God was with him* (Acts 10: 38). In the first church, there was no need for physicians because Jesus' power was working. Holiness is the key. *Ye shall therefore be holy, for I am holy* (Leviticus 11:45b). Jesus also said, *Nevertheless, when the Son of man cometh, shall he find faith on the earth?* (Luke 18:8b) Many churches today are judged according to their appearance or by their wealth and not so much by their fruits. How could God have changed his views concerning morality, carnality and spirituality? Could it be because man is expressing his rights instead of God's rights? Perhaps, this is why the earth is having so much troubles these days. In the book of Revelation 6:2-8, we find God responding in disapproval to man's abandonment of His rights. God does this in the form of different colored horses that he sends throughout all the earth. Each one bringing a different curse or plague to mankind; this we are experiencing today. Yes, God is expressing his disapproval on this earth.

The way some churches or religious organizations are brought into reality seems to be based on man's theologies. The type of leadership seems to condescend to sports figures, achievers in society, celebrities of some sort, or popular in some way. Is this the way God chooses his leadership? In the book of Hebrews, we can read how God chooses leadership. *God also bearing them witness, both with signs and wonders and with divers (various) miracles, and gifts of the Holy Ghost, according to his own will* (Hebrews 2:4). Here is how Jesus chose and equipped his first leadership to the world. *And when he (Jesus) had called unto him his twelve disciples, he gave them power against unclean spirits, to cast them out, and to heal all manner of sickness and all manner of disease* (Matthew 10:1).

Preaching is just not enough, otherwise God would not have given them authority over the powers of darkness, the devil. Fishermen became apostles, farmers became prophets, and workmen became evangelists. I'm persuaded that if Jesus applied for a position today in some churches that are doing so well, he would not qualify. Why? Believers have changed God's standards to fit church growth, monetary desires, and social success. **This is your 'lukewarm church!'**

Here are three testimonies to show that Jesus is the same yesterday, today and forever (Hebrews 13:8). Why testimonies? *Thy testimonies also are my delight and my counselors* (Psalm 119:24).

Here is the first testimony:

> I was drawn to these meetings through an advertisement in the
> Charisma Magazine. I saw before the surgery. They gave me laser
> surgery. After surgery, I was not able to see on this side. Then,
> they went to operate again and that was what caused me to lose
> sight on this side. I couldn't see anything. Now, I can read Jesus
> on the wall! I had gone up for prayer and Dr. Snyder prayed and
> laid hands on me; it was like someone shot right through my
> hand, and right to the top of my head. It was an excruciating
> pain that I felt. Now I have sight!

When this lady came for prayer, the Lord Jesus had me ask her if she
believed that when he spat in a person's eyes, according to John 9:6, that
they received sight. She answered "yes!" I then spat on my two thumbs,
placing them on her eyes and rebuked the spirit of blindness. She fell back
under the power of God's spirit. When she arose, she covered her one good
eye with her hand. She then started to shout, "I can read Jesus on the wall"
with the once blind eye.

Here is the second testimony:

> I am 83 years old and I know that Jesus still heals. I was invited to
> a special meeting of miracles in January. I attended the meeting
> because I wanted Jesus to heal my bowels and my aged back. After
> singing and preaching of God's word, Dr. Snyder announced,
> "anyone needing a touch from Jesus should come up for prayer."
> I went up and he prayed for me. I felt I was healed. I said, "Jesus
> has healed me." I went back again in February, when Lamb of
> God Ministry was conducting another miracle meeting. I again
> went up for prayer and, at that time, I told everyone present that

Jesus healed me at the January meeting. I then asked for prayer for my left ear since the hearing in it was almost gone. Prior to this, I had to wear a hearing aid. Just then, I could hear! I said, "Jesus has healed my ear too." I feel like a 20-year-old man. Miraculously, I could hear even as I walked away from the prayer line. Thank you Dr. Snyder for the night of miracles, where Jesus has a place to work through.

Here is the final testimony:

In July, I found myself sitting in the waiting room of a clinic, waiting for my name to be called. After numerous sinus infections, the doctor decided to do a C. A. T. scan on my head to see if infection had spread beyond the sinus cavities. Little did I know at that time how God would reveal his healing power and love in my life. The doctor called me early in the evening. The infection did not spread, but the C. A. T. scan showed a small slow growing, well defined cyst in the right anterior cranial fosse. They would need to do a follow-up study in four to six months with another scan. If it showed growth or started causing me troubles, I would have to have the cyst surgically removed. I remember thinking, why me God? I didn't want to dwell on this and got on to living my life the best I could. January, Dr. Thomas R Snyder was conducting healing services in the area. I decided to go and picked up my daughter on the way. After worship and praise reports, people got in line for prayer. Dr. Snyder prayed over each one. My turn came and I told of my healing need and the cyst. He anointed me with oil and asked if I believed that Jesus could heal me? I said "yes." He laid his hand where the cyst was and prayed. I felt a warmth in my head where the cyst was. It got warmer and started to spread through my whole body, to the point it became uncomfortably warm. I felt like I was being lifted up and lost all my strength. I fell back and the deacons held me up as Dr. Snyder finished the prayer. I broke out in a sweat as if I was wringing wet. My daughter came over and asked me if I was all right. I said "I felt the awesome power of God on me enfolding me in his healing love."

February, my follow up C. A. T. scan. The doctor took me to the room where they had my x-rays up from July and today's results. He looked at me and said, " I don't know what's happening but your cyst is disappearing!" The results of the x-rays were clearly evident. What was a well defined cyst was now a faded blur. He said, "he was surprised because he expected it to be the same."

Praise the Lord! He truly blessed me and showed me his power of healing. I thank Almighty God for his servant Dr. Thomas R Snyder and give all the glory to Jesus.

Jesus answered and said unto them, Go and show John again those things which ye do hear and see: The blind receive their sight, and the lame walk, the lepers are cleansed, and the deaf hear, the dead are raised up, and the poor have the gospel preached to them. And blessed is he whosoever shall not be offended in me (Matthew 11:4-6). John the Baptist had sent two of his disciples to ask Jesus whether he was the one (son of God) that should come or should they look for another. Isn't that remarkable that even John the Baptist had his doubts. He personally baptized Jesus, witnessed the Holy Spirit like a dove come upon him, and acknowledged that Jesus is the son of God. Nevertheless, because of present circumstances in his life, he had his doubts. You can see the answer Jesus gave him: the blind receive their sight, the deaf hear, and so on. Jesus still gives the same answer today through his representatives.

So many lukewarm churches today are giving out wholesale salvations. "Say this prayer and you will be saved." Working on emotions, sometimes fanaticism. When Jesus forgave sins, he did it with power and authority. We can read in Matthew 9:5-7, *Jesus said, For whether is easier, to say, Thy sins be forgiven thee; or to say, Arise, and walk? But that ye may know that the Son of man hath power on earth to forgive sins, (then saith he to the sick of the palsy,) Arise, take up thy bed, and go unto thine house. And he arose, and departed to his house.* So, you see that the forgiving of sins and the authority of God to do miracles are inseparable.

When Jesus gave this power to remit or to retain sins, it could not be received without the Holy Ghost. *And when he (Jesus) had said this, he breathed on them, and said unto them, Receive ye the Holy Ghost: whose soever sins ye remit, they are remitted unto them; and whose soever sins ye retain, they are retained* (John 20:22-23). For where the Holy Ghost is, there will be power! This is hand in glove. You will not have one without the other. This is how the early church, who Jesus personally hand-picked, remitted sins. Read Acts 2: 43.

Are these features still alive in today's true church? Has Jesus given this authority also to you? Our next chapter titled, 'Children of Light: The True Church,' will bring illumination, empowering the mind!

CHAPTER 6

Children of Light:
The True Church

It is impossible for the child of light to miss the rapture or not to know when it will take place. How can I make this profound statement? Once again God's word proclaims this very fact! *But ye, brethren, are not in darkness, that that day should overtake you as a thief. Ye are all the children of light, and the children of the day: we are not of the night, nor of darkness* (1 Thessalonians 5:4&5). We will explore in depth this immutable truth, that the children of light will not be caught as a thief in the night, in the chapter titled, Raptured! In the Twinkle of the Eye!

I would like to establish our reference point once again, the Bible, which is the word of God. *For ever, O Lord, thy word is settled in heaven* (Psalm 119:89). In this scripture, we find that the word of God is immovable, unbreakable, and enforceable forever by the awesome power of God. You can depend on it, trust it, believe in it, and experience God's reality by it.

The first recorded words that Jesus spoke after he was filled with the Holy Ghost are found in the gospel of Matthew. *But he (Jesus) answered and said, It is written, Man shall not live by bread alone, but by every word that proceedeth out of the mouth of God* (Matthew 4:4). As you live by the word of God and not by the elements of this world, you will walk in the light of the word, even as he is in the light. This is our shield and buckler. The cleansing fire of God. Satan and all the powers of darkness must yield!

On the first day of creation, God created light. *And God said, Let there be light: and there was light* (Genesis 1:3). This was the very first thing God created. The sun and the moon were created on the fourth day of creation. *And God made two great lights; the greater light to rule the day, and the lesser light to rule the night: he made the stars also* (Genesis 1:16). This first light that God created did not receive it's source from the sun or the moon. They were both non-existent in creation. *Then spake Jesus again unto them, saying, I am the light of the world: he that followeth me shall not walk in darkness, but shall have the light of life* (John 8:12). This is the light that fills all and all, every molecule of our being; physical, intellectual, and spiritual. This light that Almighty God created framed the backdrop to all His future creations when he said, 'let there be light.' This is the same light that Father God uses to create sons and daughters today. When one becomes enlightened to the scriptures that Jesus is the Savior, the great physician, the great provider; eternal life itself; they have found this light themselves becoming a child of light. *For in him we live, and move, and have our being; as certain also of your own poets have said, For we are also his offspring* (Acts 17: 28). Here is a parable that will help.

A King who was very wise had three sons. He knew that someday he would have to relinquish his kingdom to one of his sons. He wanted to choose the one that would most reflect himself. So, he devised a test that would reveal his desires. Here was the test. He had a very large room; it was tremendous! He said to each of his sons that he would give them the sum of five hundred dollars. With this money, they would purchase items or materials that would best fill the room. The son who would be the wisest would best fill the room; therefore being declared the victor, the next King. The second and third sons were quick to take the money and go out and buy objects that would accomplish their desired purpose. They both looked to physical resources to fill the room. The first son, however, after deep thought and meditation required only a small portion of the supplied amount, five dollars to be exact. This brought the attention not only of the King but all his subjects. The second son came first and brought into the room feathers. He spread the feathers in all directions. They mounted up high on the walls. However, there still remained open space. The third son brought in straw. Again, a very large portion of the room was filled with his solution. His limited funds, however, caused the situation to cry out for more straw.

Being that his two brothers had already failed in their attempts, there was much excitement and talk concerning the first son. Could he be the next king? After all, someone would have to be King. In time, people started to lose interest. They reasoned among themselves that something must have gone amiss. Perhaps, this was only a façade of showmanship and a unique demonstration of trickery. They couldn't imagine how the first son, only in possession of five dollars, could do what his brothers failed.

After all, their sum was a hundred times greater. When least expected, in came the first son. Out of his pocket came a candle and a match. Placing the candle on the floor in the center of the room, he lit the match, and **The whole room was filled with light!**

Now the choice was easy; wisdom had chosen the next King. Under the conditions given, only two things could have filled that room: darkness or light. The darkness was already there. The light had to be purchased through wisdom. Jesus is the wisdom of God and our King. *But unto them which are called, both Jews and Greeks, Christ the power of God, and the wisdom of God* (1 Corinthians 1:24). Again we can read: *But of him are ye in Christ Jesus, who of God is made unto us wisdom, and righteousness, and sanctification, and redemption* (1 Corinthians 1:30).

When Almighty God created light in the first chapter of Genesis verse three, we find that darkness first appears in verse four. When man (Adam and Eve) was ushered out of God's presence (the garden of Eden and the tree of life), man lost that light, retaining only the darkness. So what happened to that marvelous light that all creation was founded on? John the Baptist said that he was not that light, but Jesus was that light. *That was the true Light, which lighteth every man that cometh into the world* (John 1:9). This light does not receive it's energy source from the sun or the moon. This light, in essence, is truly the love of God, his very breath! When he spoke *This is my beloved son, in whom I am well pleased* (Matthew 3:17), Father God has now given that light a name, Jesus. Not only is Jesus that true light, but he also is the only hope for mankind. *For ye were sometimes darkness, but now are ye light in the Lord: walk as children of light* (Ephesians 5:8). Here is how you will know the true church, which is the body of Christ; all the children of light will want to bring their deeds before God. They will be able to stand in His light because their deeds are not darkness. Walking or living in darkness is the same as blindness. How can the blind lead the blind? They will both fall into a ditch. *For all that is in the world, the lust of the flesh, and the lust of the eyes, and the pride of life, is not of the father, but is of the world* (1 John 2:16). God would have all man come to this light and be saved. *Who will have all men to be saved, and to come unto the knowledge of the truth* (1 Timothy 2: 4). All have to deal with the darkness of the devil who has blinded the eyes of all mankind to the goodness of God. *And this is the condemnation, that light is come into the world, and men loved darkness rather than light, because their deeds were evil* (John 3:19).

No matter how well the intentions of men are, they are limited to the elements that are in the world and the limitations of their abilities. Here is a testimony that will reveal the limitations of man and the unlimited abilities of God.

I am giving this testimony for the miracle God has done in my life. I give all the glory to God and praise to Jesus Christ;

thanking him for hearing the prayers of deliverance that Dr. Thomas R Snyder offered on my behalf.

About one year ago I began to have major stomach pains. I would daily get sharp stomach pains. They began to get so bad, to the point that on certain occasions it would bring me to my knees. My mom would call Dr. Snyder for prayers. After he prayed the pain would cease. Then a few days later it would start up again.

My mom and I decided to seek medical attention. When the visit was over, I was told to track what I ate and avoid what gives me pain, after I have eaten. I was told to take this and take that; to do this and don't do that. I started to realize it was going to be a test of faith.

I was cut off of dairy and greasy foods. Some time had passed and more issues arose. I had internal bleeding and sought relief from gastrologist, gynecolgist and medical practitioners. The pain increased, I began to lose weight and other issues arose. I continued to seek God for help through Dr. Snyder's counseling and prayers. Miracles began to happen one after another.

After Dr. Snyder rebuked the spirit that was holding me, the internal bleeding immediately stopped! I had been battling this for one long year. Next, the upper and lower stomach pain slowly began to cease. Then, one day I decided I wanted to have a glass of milk. Not only did it taste great, but it didn't make me sick. So just to test the waters, I went out the next day and had a giant milkshake. It was a miracle. Not one bit of pain!

I am so thankful to Dr. Thomas R Snyder for all his prayers and making the Bible real. I was just like the woman with the issue of blood, who spent all her money on doctors and one day Jesus healed me.

Children of light will always be victorious. The devil, sickness, pain and all other powers of darkness that are in one's life **must go in the name of Jesus!**

There are avenues that Father God has given to the child of light to receive this authoritative power. One way is by the laying on of hands. *Wherefore I put thee in remembrance that thou stir up the gift of God, which is in thee by the putting on of hands. For God has not given us the spirit of fear; but of power, and of love, and of a sound mind* (2 Timothy 1:6 & 7). Here are three men of God who over the years have laid hands on this author, conferring this authoritative power.

Dr. D. G. S. Dhinakaran, author of many books, founder of Jesus Calls Ministries and Karunya University Madrais, India (now under the spiritual leadership of his son Dr. Paul Dhinakaran).

Rev. George Stormont, author of the book '*Wigglesworth, A Man Who Walked with God*'.

Rev. A. J. Rowden, founder of Evangelistic Center Church at Kansas City, Missouri, also his biography '*EN ROUTE TO Worshiping in the Spirit*'.

All three of these men of God have gone on to be with the Lord. As you can see by the testimonies in this publication, when a man or woman of God speaks, not one word will fall to the ground. *And Samuel grew, and the Lord was with him, and did let none of his words fall to the ground* (1 Samuel 3:19). Yes! This is one way that Almighty God confers his authority to his servants. Just as he did through these 'men of God' to myself.

Jesus was the word made flesh. *And the Word was made flesh, and dwelt among us, (and we beheld his glory, the glory as of the only begotten of the*

Father), full of grace and truth (John 1:14). As we shared earlier, He is that true light that came into the world. Therefore, the word is another source of this true light to unlock the authority and power of God. *Thy word is a lamp unto my feet, and a light unto my path* (Psalm 119:105). Always remember, it is God's good pleasure to give us the kingdom. *Jesus said, Fear not, little flock; for it is your Father's good pleasure to give you the kingdom* (Luke 12:32). There is no darkness at all in God's word. *Being born again, not of corruptible seed, but of incorruptible, by the word of God, which liveth and abided forever* (1 Peter 1:23).

Jesus commissioned Paul (and the true church) *To open their eyes, and to turn them from darkness to light, and from the power of Satan unto God, that they may receive forgiveness of sins, and inheritance among them which are sanctified by faith that is in me* (Jesus)(Acts 26:18). This enlightening of the scriptures will guide you as you earnestly covet the best gifts. It will also instruct all to this paramount revelation, that charity (love) is the most excellent way. *But covet earnestly the best gifts: and yet shew I unto you a more excellent way* (1 Corinthians 12:31). In the chapter titled, 'Lovest Thou Me?' these treasures will surface.

Why does Father God equip His true saints of light with these gifts? Are they to be used for personal gain or enjoyment? Jesus imparted these gifts to the first church and still imparts them today. In our next chapter titled, **'Boldness and Exploits'**, like manna from heaven, God will satisfy even the hungriest of souls.

Chapter 7

'Boldness and Exploits'

The people that do know their God shall be strong, and do exploits (Daniel 11:32b). There is a holy boldness that will accompany the true believer. Without debate, every time God worked his divine will on this earth, He chose holy boldness to be the main ingredient. In order to attain this main ingredient, you must receive the Holy Ghost. Here are some examples of this truth.

One day, out of the blue, John the Baptist decided to start baptizing in the Jordan River for the remission of sins. This not only was a bold decision on his behalf, but he started a new religion that still receives God's approval today. Was this his decision or was he moved by another source which empowered him with this holy boldness? *And John bare record, saying, I saw the Spirit descending from heaven like a dove, and it abode upon him.(Jesus) And I knew him not: but **he** that sent me to baptize with water, the same said unto me, Upon whom thou shall see the spirit descending, and remaining on him, the same is he which baptizeth with the Holy Ghost* (John 1: 32 & 33). Just who was this **'he'** who sent me (John) to baptize? This **'he'** also had knowledge of who the son of God was and how God would reveal him to the whole world? **It was the Holy Ghost!** *For he (John the Baptist) shall be great in the sight of the Lord, and shall drink neither wine nor strong drink;*

and he shall be filled with the Holy Ghost, even from his mother's womb (Luke 1: 15). This holy boldness can only come from the Holy Ghost.

Moses was moved by this boldness when he went before Pharaoh, demanding the release of God's people. Noah was moved by this boldness when he believed God and took the bold step to build the ark, trusting God for the provision of the waters. The apostle Paul possessed this boldness when he declared the gospel to the Gentiles. Peter and John possessed this boldness when they witnessed before the high priest Annas.

The early church knew exactly the source of this boldness. *And now, Lord, behold, their threatenings: and grant unto thy servants, that with all boldness they may speak thy word, by stretching forth thine hand to heal; and that signs and wonders may be done by the name of thy holy child Jesus* (Acts 4: 29 & 30). It's interesting that the early church knew that it was the hand of God that did the healings and the signs and wonders. Without being filled with the Holy Ghost and using the matchless name of Jesus, they knew nothing would happen. *But ye shall receive power, after the Holy Ghost is come upon you: and ye shall be witnesses unto me both in Jerusalem, and in all Judea, and in Samaria, and unto the uttermost part of the earth* (Acts 1:8).

Here is a testimony, in her own words, that will confirm this fact today.

I was born and raised in a strong Catholic family. Twelve years of Catholic school and a 'Catholic attitude' toward religion.

In my mid twenties, I started to see that I was empty inside and had no real connection with God. I knew all the Bible stories, but I just never could connect them to my busy lifestyle.

I started searching other religions, even some cults, but I never found what I was looking for.

I was diagnosed with a very serious form of cancer and would probably not live very long. At that time, I became very angry with God and completely immersed myself in my work and family; believing no loving God could be so cruel to a 'good' person like myself.

For five years, I remained busy and pretty free of any serious health problems, but still very angry at God.

Then, last February, I became very ill with migraine headaches and loss of vision. I couldn't work. The doctors did brain surgery and told me the cancer had spread through my body, my brain and I had less than six months to live.

While I was in the hospital, I was visited daily by a wonderful priest who helped me feel the love of God and opened a door that had been closed for a long time.

For the next four months, I had been waiting to die; since the doctors had told me I would die suddenly from an inter-cranial hemorrhage, due to the cancer near my carotid artery.

The son of my best friend started talking to me about this wonderful Lord he had found at the Lamb of God Church. Since I had seen him grow up and seen the remarkable changes in his life, I figured there must be something very powerful in what he was saying. So I went.

I was sitting there enjoying the singing and uplifting prayers, when all of a sudden, I was encouraged to go up for prayer. I can't explain how I felt! I was afraid and wasn't too sure about any of this.

I don't remember everything, but I do remember Dr. Snyder saying not to be afraid. When he put his hands on my head, I felt the most strange, warm and wonderful sensation throughout my body. I believe that was the beginning of my healing. I felt a warm closeness to God, I had never felt before. I also have to add, that I was wearing a wig due to radiation. So, I prayed to God to heal me, but please don't let Dr. Snyder knock the wig off! I still laugh about that. I have never worn a wig for prayer since.

Today I am well past the doctors predicted final days and I feel better than I have in a long time.

Jesus has worked through Dr. Snyder and healed my vision, given me strength, and taken a large lump out of my breast. He has healed me and given me the ability to hope, thank and glorify him. In the process, I have found a warm, caring, and loving family that I have needed for so long in the church.

My prayer today is that God will give Dr. Thomas R Snyder the strength and courage to keep doing the Lord's work. To keep me close to him and never ever let me think that I don't need the Lord in my life again.

The early church prayed that with all boldness they may speak his word, by stretching forth thine hand to heal, and that signs and wonders may be done by the name of thy holy child Jesus. This is exactly how

•

this testimony is reality today. This boldness is for all believers. Don't sell yourself short! You have the word of God as your undisputable foundation. *Then Peter said unto them, Repent, and be baptized every one of you in the name of Jesus Christ for the remission of sins, and ye shall receive the gift of the Holy Ghost* (Acts 2: 38).

When I was in Jerusalem some years ago, the Lord opened up many doors for His Majesty and Glory. In the process of time, as we were fellowshipping in the spirit, a beloved brother stood up and spoke this by the Holy Ghost: " when anyone stretches forth their hand, in the name of Jesus, it no longer was their hand, but the hand of God." This boldness is established in faith and trust that **God will perform his word**. Only the Holy Ghost can give this divinely appointed **'boldness.'** So powerful is this boldness that not only will it make you as the master (Jesus) in this world, but be demonstrated on that day of judgment. *Herein is our love made perfect, that we may have boldness in the day of judgment: because as he is, so are we in this world* (1 John 4: 17).

Too many people today, because of their lack of knowledge, are looking at the evil in the world instead of the word of God for His timetable. In the chapter titled 'Raptured! In the Twinkle of the Eye,' we will expound on God's timetable concerning all future events.

As we shared earlier, God will always have a bold forerunner to reveal his will before he performs it in the earth. God will do nothing until these two scriptures are fulfilled. *Surely the Lord God will do nothing, but he revealth his secret unto his servants the prophets* (Amos 3:7). *So thou, O son of man, I have set thee a watchman unto the house of Israel; therefore thou shalt hear the word at my mouth, and warn them from me* (Ezekiel 33:7).

Boldness without exploits is dead even as faith without works is dead. *Even so faith, if it hath not works, is dead, being alone* (James 2:17). The definition of exploits is this: a bold and unusual act; a daring deed. Jeremiah said that the word burned within his heart. *Then I said, I will not make mention of him, nor speak any more in his name. But his word was in my heart as a burning fire shut up in my bones, and I was weary with forbearing, and I could not stay* (Jeremiah 20:9). He could not contain it's awesome power.

He had to bring it forth for all to hear. The Saints waited in the upper room and continued in prayer, all receiving the pouring out of the Holy Ghost. Yes, this too was a burning. For the spirit of God represented himself as cloven tongues of fire. *And there appeared unto them cloven tongues like as of fire, and it sat upon each of them* (Acts 2:3). A greater depth into this pouring out of the Holy Ghost will be shared in the chapter titled, Early and Latter Rain: 'The Second Pentecost.'

So, we find ourselves with this conclusion, that the Holy Ghost will give to all believers boldness, and a burning desire to perform exploits in Jesus' name.

Jesus asked Peter this question, "Lovest Thou Me?" In our next chapter titled, 'Lovest Thou Me?' the very heart and soul of God will emerge.

CHAPTER 8

Lovest Thou Me?

Many people today are worried about the end of the world, the rapture, the tribulation, the Antichrist, the economy or just the future in general, concerning this world we live in. The only antidote to resolve this weariness of mind is **'LOVE!'**

*He that loveth not knoweth not God; for **God is love!*** (1 John 4:8). This is the centerpiece of the Christian faith. This love is the birthplace of our Lord and Savior Jesus. It is the root and the offspring of David. Nothing can separate the true believer from it's source. *For I am persuaded, that neither death, nor life, nor angels, nor principalities, nor powers, nor things present, Nor things to come, nor height, nor depth, nor any other creature, shall be able to separate us from the love of God, which is in Christ Jesus our Lord* (Romans 8:38-39).

Many believers see this love as a one-way street. God's love for them only. "Give me this God." "I need your help God." "I want, what I want God!" How can love be exalted and brought to the pinnacle of perfection when it is only one sided? Peter had dialect with Jesus just before he ascended into heaven to sit at the right hand of God. The purpose of this communication between Jesus and Peter was a commissioning of Peter to replace him in his physical absence. *And I say also unto thee, That thou art*

Peter, and upon this rock I will build my church; and the gates of hell shall not prevail against it (Matthew 16:18). Can you imagine the scene? The temptation, the crucifixion, the three days in the tomb, and finally the resurrection from the dead were all behind them. The precarious work of the cross was all finished! God was very pleased with Jesus' fulfilling of all the scriptures; so pleased, that His spirit rose him from the dead. Jesus, who had been given all authority in the earth, would now pass the baton. Three words were all that was necessary, **"Lovest thou me!"**

With these three words, the authority, victory of the cross, and power over all darkness was conferred to the church. With this love, Jesus becomes the head of the body of believers which supplies God's endless love, through his matchless name, to a lost, dark, and dying world. *For God so loved the world that he gave his only begotten son, that whosoever believeth in him should not perish, but have everlasting life* (John 3:16). Love was and still is the catalyst for motivation that completes the essence of life: not a natural or sensual love, but it must be the love of God.

Here are two testimonies that will reveal that God's love is a two-way street. Both testimonies are given in their own words.

First testimony:

> I went up for prayer. It was very powerful and I couldn't resist
> and I didn't fight back.

> I whispered to Dr. Snyder, "the devil is trying to destroy me."
> That's the only thing I said. Whatever it is, I've been through a
> lot of spiritual battles. Evil is trying to destroy me.

> As Dr. Snyder laid hands on me and began to pray, I felt the
> Holy Spirit move. It's not an emotion but when the Holy Spirit
> filled me, tears came to my eyes. I was slain in the spirit. Nothing

pushed me. Not a human force. It's the spirit. I don't lie down, that's because my whole system shuts down within one minute. I stop breathing! I was lying down, under the power of the Holy Spirit, for 4 to 5 minutes and I open my eyes. I looked puzzled. Everything was fine. I didn't expect that miracle. I didn't ask for it but God gave me wholeness. This room is full of the Holy Spirit.

I thank God for Dr. Thomas R Snyder's ministry and give all the glory to Jesus!

Second testimony:

I attended the meeting Saturday morning at my nursing home where I reside. I asked for prayer at the beginning of the program because of all the pain in my body on the whole left side. I felt I would not be able to stay. As Dr. Snyder prayed over me, the Lord Jesus shared that I should sing during the worship and the pain would leave. As one of the worship songs was being sung, Jesus was faithful and all the pain left my body not to return.

I thank Almighty God and give the glory to Jesus who healed me. The song was 'Power in the Blood.' This truly proves that Jesus has power to heal.

Once again we can see the love of God being poured out on his lambs and sheep. It's interesting to see that in both of these testimonies they received more than they asked for, especially in the first testimony. He was overwhelmed with amazement because he received from Jesus Christ much more than he expected. These sheep were hungrier than they realized.

This is how God's love works when it's a two-way street. The believer must be willing to feed the world with God's love. Here is the commission Jesus personally gave to Peter and all believers who love his appearing. *So when they had dined, Jesus saith to Simon Peter, Simon, son of Jonas, lovest thou me more than these? He saith unto him, Yea, Lord; thou knowest that I love thee. He saith unto him, **Feed my lambs**. He saith to him again the second time, Simon, son of Jonas, lovest thou me? He saith unto him, Yea, Lord; thou knowest that I love thee. He saith unto him, **Feed my sheep**. He saith unto him the third time, Simon, son of Jonas, lovest thou me? Peter was grieved because he said unto him the third time, Lovest thou me? And he said unto him, Lord, thou knowest all things; thou knowest that I love thee. Jesus saith unto him, **Feed my sheep*** (John 21:15-17).

When Peter was asked three times this question, "lovest thou me?" this was the intent, to reveal to all believers that they have the capacity to love the Lord with all their heart, soul, mind, and strength. Love never fails, when directed to God through Jesus and then to this needful world.

Earlier in this chapter, it was revealed how great a sacrifice that Jesus achieved in fulfilling the Scriptures. Here is the wisdom of God. Take a good look at what Jesus endured for all believers. Can you hear his sweet loving voice asking, **"lovest thou me?"** The heart melts as it answers, **"thou knowest I love thee!"** This is the key to the opening of Father God's heart, authority, and power-**LOVE!**

God has a heart and a soul. Here are two scriptures that will establish this fact. *And when he had removed him, he raised up unto them David to be their king; to whom also he gave testimony, and said, I have found David the son of Jesse, a man after **mine own heart**, which shall fulfill all my will* (Acts 13:22). *Now the just shall live by faith: but if any man draw back, **my soul** shall have no pleasure in him* (Hebrews 10:38). In possession of these, God has the capacity of feeling your love, even the love of your thoughts. *But when Jesus perceived their thoughts, he answering said unto them, What reason* *ye in your hearts?* (Luke 5:22) At this very moment all of your thoughts are before God. Jesus will never keep back any good thing from his favored children. Yes, even in our thoughts, we are able to please him.

Pleasing is the qualified results desired by love. Jesus said that he always pleased God. *And he that sent me is with me: the Father has not left me alone; for I do always those things that please him* (John 8:29). There are many benefits in pleasing God. Here are two that come to mind. *And whatsoever we ask, we receive of him, because we keep his commandments, and do those things that are pleasing in his sight* (1 John 3:22). This benefit is intended by God to be realized in this world on a daily basis. It is dynamic in purpose, unlimited by design, and completely satisfying. Secondly, pleasing God champions the hurdle of being left behind. Enoch pleased God and God took (raptured) him. As the true believer heeds this instruction 'lovest thou me,' God will be pleased, qualifying him or her for the rapture. Also conferring the power and authority that Jesus himself demonstrated while on earth.

Is there a second Pentecost on the horizon? Does the word of God confirm or deny this future event? The next chapter titled, Early and Latter Rain: 'The Second Pentecost' will resolve any doubts.

CHAPTER 9

Early and Latter Rain: 'The Second Pentecost'

All over the world, the body of Christ is crying out to Almighty God, their Heavenly Father, for more of the Holy Ghost. Iniquity is abounding and there is a stir in the hearts of all saints. Could this be the forerunner of the latter rain? In order to grasp the importance of the times we are in, we must first establish whether God has ordained a ladder rain, a second Pentecost.

So unshakable is the word of God, rich with wisdom and knowledge that we only need to reach out with our faith to be filled to satisfaction. In our previous chapter titled 'Lovest Thou Me?' it was established that the true saint of God would love Him with all their heart, soul, mind, and strength. Enlightened to this fact confirms that one day they could be raptured and forever be with the Lord. These next two scriptures, will reveal that there will be a latter rain or second pouring of the Holy Ghost. *And it shall come to pass, if ye shall hearken diligently unto my commandments which I command you this day, to love the Lord your God, and to serve him with all your heart and with all your soul, That I will give you the rain of your land in his due season, the first rain and the latter rain, that thou mayest gather in thy corn, and thy wine, and thine oil* (Deuteronomy 11:13-14).

The sole purpose of the latter rain is for a gathering in or an in gathering of the harvest of the earth. This is a spiritual harvest of souls. *And another angel came out of the temple, crying with a loud voice to him that sat on the cloud, Thrust in thy sickle, and reap: for the time is come for thee to reap; for the harvest of the earth is ripe* (Revelation 14:15). This is the whole purpose of the latter rain, the pouring out of the Holy Ghost on all flesh, so God can receive many sons and daughters to glory.

The first rain that was experienced on the day of Pentecost was poured out on approximately one hundred and twenty believers. *And in those days Peter stood up in the midst of the disciples, and said, (the number of names together were about an hundred and twenty)* (Acts 1:15). That was the first or early rain. This next or latter rain will be poured out on all flesh! Anyone and everyone who is associated with the Lord Jesus in anyway, will receive the spirit. This will be a universal outpouring of the Holy Spirit. *The earth shall be full of the knowledge of the Lord, as the waters cover the sea* (Isaiah 11:9b). There will be miracles, signs and wonders all over the world. Many, many, many representatives of Jesus will convince the world not only that he exists, but has truly risen from the dead, and is Lord of Lords, and King of Kings. What a harvest it will be! *The glory of this latter house shall be greater than of the former, saith the Lord of hosts: and in this place will I give peace, saith the Lord of hosts* (Haggai 2:9).

In order to understand how the Lord will be able to pour out his spirit on both carnal and spiritual believers, we must take a close look at two Kings: King Saul and King David.

There is a most interesting event that happened in King Saul's life. He was fulfilling the will of God until he took matters into his own hands, altering God's word. His patience being tried, he gave into the beggarly elements of this world. Instead of following the word of God he interpreted or altered it to fit natural desires. *And Samuel said, What hast thou done? And Saul said, Because I saw that the people were scattered from me, and that thou camest not within the days appointed, and that the Philistines gathered themselves together at Mich mash; Therefore said I, the Philistines will come down now upon me to Gilgal, and I have not made supplication unto the Lord: I forced myself therefore, and offered a burnt offering. And Samuel said to Saul, Thou has done foolishly: thou hast not kept the commandment of the Lord thy God, which he commanded thee: for now would the Lord have established thy kingdom upon Israel for ever* (1Samuel 13:11-13). So many religious organizations and churches have changed the word of God and replaced it with their abilities to get what they desire. Calling it all God as King Saul did. This is a very dangerous position. It doesn't matter how successful of a religious façade before man's eyes; to God, it is all shameful and nakedness. Then the unthinkable happens, God removes the Holy Spirit from off of King Saul and replaces the Holy Spirit with an evil spirit. The Holy Spirit is then sent to David, the shepherd boy. *Then Samuel took the horn of oil, and anointed him (David) in the midst of his brethren: and* **the Spirit of the Lord came upon David** *from that day forward. So Samuel rose up and went to Ramah. But* **the Spirit of the Lord departed from Saul, and an evil spirit from the Lord troubled him** (1 Samuel 16:13-14).

Here is a testimony, in this young man's words, that will show how he inquired of God; and the Lord did answer.

> I had an infected ingrown toenail for six months. The ingrown toenail gave me so much pain that it was hard for me to even walk. I went to the doctor four times. Each time to calm the infection, but the infection just kept getting worse. It got so bad that when I took off my shoe, there was blood and puss stains on my sock.
>
> Finally the doctor told me he was going to remove the ingrown toenail with the infection. The reason he didn't do that in the

first place was the anesthetic doesn't work with the infection. So I felt all the pain when he was removing the ingrown toenail. The infection never went away and the ingrown toenail grew back. This surgery was repeated three times and the same condition persisted. However, this time I went for a healing from God.

Dr. Snyder prayed over me and the Lord Jesus showed him to tell me *not to put anything on that toe*! That night, I left my toe alone. Within two weeks. I notice that my toe wasn't bleeding or pussing. A week after that, the infection was healed. The ingrown toenail wasn't so painful. A week later, the ingrown toenail was gone! Eight months of doctors and they couldn't heal it. Something that big could never heal itself. **That toe was healed by God!**

I give all the glory to Jesus, who so mercifully felt my pain and healed my toe. Thank you Dr. Thomas R Snyder for using the gifts of the Holy Spirit.

You could almost imagine, this young man, just like David sitting down and writing a most wonderful Psalm. Why do I say this? I can hear the conviction of his heart, when he concludes his testimony. So aware that it was God who heard his pain, suffering and tears, as he shouts, **"That toe was healed by God!"**

So, King Saul is now plagued by an evil spirit, and David is now in the possession of the Holy Spirit. Saul is still the king. Having all the natural resources at his disposal, it still looks as if God is with him. However, because of the evil spirit on him, through jealousy and envy, he pursues David relentlessly. Then God does a most remarkable thing, **He puts his Holy Spirit on King Saul !** Here is Saul with evil in his heart, yet God is able to put the Holy Spirit on him. *And he (Saul) went thither to Naioth in Ramah: and the Spirit of God was upon him also, and he went on, and prophesied, until he came to Naioth in Ramah. And he stripped off his clothes also, and prophesied before Samuel in like manner, and lay down naked all that day and all that night. Wherefore they say, Is Saul also among the prophets?* (1 Samuel 19:23-24).

Here we are experiencing that all things are possible with God. David was trapped by evil. King Saul was determined to destroy him. By God putting His Holy Spirit on Saul, David, then was able to escape his grips. There is a great tribulation coming on this earth. God has designed the latter rain for a witness to offer a way to escape the coming events. God will witness to the whole world whom Jesus is. This must be done with the Holy Ghost and power. God will not allow anyone who professes to know Jesus but are workers of iniquity (like King Saul was) to prohibit Him from offering His love and mercies to the whole human race, before He begins the tribulation. He shows here that he will place his Spirit both on the carnal and spiritual believer to get His business accomplished, just like he did with King Saul. Here are some Scriptures that will enforce this conclusion: *Thou hast ascended on high, thou hast led captivity captive: thou hast received gifts for men;* **yea, for the rebellious also**, *that the Lord God might dwell among men* (Psalm 68:18). Again, in the gospel of Matthew: *Not every one that saith unto me, Lord, Lord, shall enter into the kingdom of heaven; but he that doeth the will of my Father which is in heaven. Many will say to me in that day, Lord, Lord, have we not prophesied in thy name? and in thy name have cast out devils? and in thy name done many wonderful works? And then will I profess unto them, I never knew you: depart from me, ye that work iniquity* (Matthew 7:21-23).

In the early rain, Pentecost, there was only good seed in the soil. When evil seed or tares tried to come in with Ananias and Sapphira, Acts 5:1-10, not even one lie could stand before the Holy Ghost. Among today's believers, you hear of adulteries, financial misuse, and many other ungodly principles being exercised almost daily. Lying seems to be almost common place. God will always have his faithful! This time with the good seed is a lot of bad seed. Therefore, the pouring of the Holy Spirit will spill out to all that are in God's garden, both on the obedient and disobedient. There are many vessels, some for honor and some for dishonor. *But in a great house, there are not only vessels of gold and of silver, but also of wood and of earth; and some to honor, and some to dishonor* (2 Timothy 2:20).

Jesus is wanting to give the latter rain and see the precious fruit be taken to heaven. *Behold, the husbandman waiteth for the precious fruit of the earth, and hath long patience for it, until he receive the early and latter rain* (James 5:7). Jesus is wanting to do it all!

In the chapter titled 'Raptured! In the Twinkle of the Eye,' the evidence will surface to why the Holy Ghost must be poured out as a chief ingredient associated with the rapture.

On the cover of this book, the word tribulation appears. This in turn brings up the subject of the antichrist. Who is he and what is this number 666? Our next chapter titled, Tribulation, Antichrist, '666' will unmask all the devil's disguises and dispel any mysteries surrounding God's timetable of future events.

CHAPTER 10

Tribulation, Antichrist, '666'

Volumes have been written concerning the antichrist, the number '666,' and the events concerning the tribulation. Jesus himself gives us some very encouraging enlightenment concerning this entire subject. He said that **it will be impossible for the true believer to be deceived!** The confirmation is found in the gospel of Matthew. *For there shall arise false Christs , and false prophets, and shall shew great signs and wonders; insomuch that, if it were possible, they shall deceive the very elect* (Matthew 24:24). The elect are the children of light; God's Saints in this world. It's not so much who is the antichrist or is he on earth today, but your relationship with God. This is the only safe haven in these troublous times. This births the question, "Is there a devil?"

The devil has been given three distinct names in the Bible; they are Lucifer, Satan, and the devil. There are many other referenced names used towards his character; however, these are the most universal.

The first name he was given is Lucifer, which means, 'the morning Star.' He walked before God in heaven, and God put his affection on him until iniquity was found in him. *How art thou fallen from heaven, O Lucifer, son of the morning! how art thou cut down to the ground, which didst weaken the nations! For thou hast said in thine heart, I will ascend into heaven, I will exalt my throne above the stars of God: I will sit also upon the mount of the congregation, in the sides of the north: I will ascend above the heights of the clouds; I will be like the most High. Yet thou shalt be brought down to hell, to the sides of the pit* (Isaiah 14:12-15). What happened then? We find God's response to all of this in the gospel of Luke. *And he (Jesus) said unto them, I beheld Satan as lightning fall from heaven* (Luke 10:18). By Jesus saying this, he revealed two precious jewels of revelation. First, that Almighty God changed Lucifer's name to Satan. Also, God changed Satan's dwelling place. God will change Satan's dwelling place yet two more times: when he is cast down to the earth and, finally, when he is cast into the lake of fire, HELL! It's very important to understand that Satan has not yet been cast down to this earth. Later in this chapter, we will pinpoint this event.

The second name given is Satan. The meaning of this name is 'opponent or arch enemy of good.' The first appearance of this name in the Bible is in 1 Chronicles 21:1. In earlier chapters of the Bible, his dastardly deeds were disguised under different names such as 'the serpent,' 'Baal,' and so on. To examine just how Satan influences mankind, as per say, the book of Job shouts volumes of declaration. Here we see Satan, going to and fro in the earth, seeking whom he can devour. Job gets mixed up with Satan not on his own accord but by God permitting Satan to try him. The case is a simple one. God was watching over Job by hedging him in with his protective love. Job was prospering and enjoying the blessings of God. Satan puts this question before God, "Does Job really have a fear of God? If Job was to receive some troubles, instead of good things, he would curse God to his face." This test would truly show Job's heart, settling the matter once and for all! Satan had hoped that Job would fail and abandon God. Here are the Scriptures pertaining to this event. *Now there was a day when the sons of God came to present themselves before the Lord, and Satan came also among them. And the Lord said unto Satan, Whence comest thou? Then Satan answered the Lord, and said, From going to and fro in the earth, and from walking up and down in it. And the Lord said unto Satan, Hast thou considered my servant Job, that there is none like him in the earth, a perfect and an upright man, one that feareth God, and escheweth evil? Then Satan answered the Lord, and said, Doth Job fear God for nought? Hast not thou made an hedge about him, and about his house, and about all that he hath on every side? Thou hast blessed the work of his hands, and his substance is increased in the land. But put forth thine hand now, and touch all that he hath, and he will curse thee to thy face. And the Lord said unto Satan, Behold, all that he hath is in thy power; only upon himself put not forth thine hand. So Satan went forth from the presence of the Lord* (Job 1:6-12). It is imperative to grasp the fact that there is nothing good in Satan. No matter how he presents himself to you; through people, situations, or events, his only desires are to rend, steal, destroy, and kill. The only protection anyone can have against his powers of darkness are in Jesus Christ. Don't be deceived! The battle belongs to the Lord!

The third name given is the devil, which means traducer or false accuser. All three names are given to the same person, however this one seems to be the most common. In the King James version of the Bible, the name devil does not appear in the Old Testament. Why? The Messiah or son of God had not yet come in the flesh. This name change signifies the fact that Lucifer, alias Satan, will never accept that Jesus is the son of God and that he has come in the flesh. His new name first appears in the book of Matthew chapter four, when the devil tempts Jesus in the wilderness. The devil keeps asking Jesus if he is the son of God, living up to his new name.

There could be some confusion concerning the person of the devil. Jesus at one point casts out a legion of devils. Mary Magdalene had seven devils cast out of her. Can they all be the same person? In the book of Jude, we find the answer. *And the angels which kept not their first estate, but left their own habitation, he hath reserved in everlasting chains under darkness unto the judgment of the great day* (Jude 6). Yes, Lucifer was cast out of heaven and so were a third of the angels (Revelation 12: 4). So clever and cunning is his voice that even

God's holy angels were swayed. Therefore, the title devil is given to any spirit not confessing Jesus has come in the flesh. *And every spirit that confesseth not that Jesus Christ is come in the flesh is not of God: and this is that spirit of antichrist, whereof ye have heard that it should come; and even now already is it in the world* (1 John 4:3). The devil will have his name changed a fourth time by the sovereign will of God to Dragon. This will be when he is cast down on the earth and enters into a human. Every time that God changed Lucifer's habitation, he changed his name also to fit the position. So also will God change the names of all that are accounted worthy to attain eternal life. This new name will fit their new habitation, which is heaven. This, will be expounded on in the chapter titled, 'The Books Were Opened.'

Here is a testimony, in his own words, that will confirm the existence of devils today.

I started seeking different purposes to life: witchcraft, positive thinking. I attended college and started seeking spirits, seeking a guide. I read many books, some on a spirit named Seth, speaking through a person. Books on reincarnation and books by Edgar Casey concerning spiritualism.

I acquired a Ouija board and demons began to communicate with me. I was hospitalized twice. At the beginning, it seemed great to be with demons. They told me I had powers as God. The demons did some small signs, and made me think I did them. However, in no time at all, I just sat in a chair like a vegetable. Once they kept me in my room for five days. They wouldn't let me eat or go to the bathroom. They were making me throw up and so on. Then I tried psychics, Christian psychics, Tara cards, Crystal balls, and religious exorcists and deliverance meetings; nothing helped. I figured if there is a devil, there must be a God.

I attended a meeting sponsored by the Lamb of God Church. I was in despair, in need of deliverance. I needed the demons to be cast out of my life. Their powers and voices tried to hold me bound from allowing Dr. Snyder to pray for me. These voices in my mind spoke insults of Dr. Snyder, saying, "he had beady eyes, was a weasel and to not let him touch me. Also, if I fell down, under the power of God, they would enter my saliva and choked me to death."

As Dr. Snyder neared to pray for me, they ordered me to beat him up. As I am much larger than him, this was a reasonable request. They also went on to say that Dr. Snyder was a false prophet. There were six or seven demons in me, four of whom I knew by name: Vispain, Courtney, Scottie, and Irish. As hands were laid on me, Dr. Snyder said, "Jesus is sending the Devils away and the Holy Ghost is coming into your body." I went out cold under the power of God for 3 to 5 minutes. When I awoke, I heard the demon's voice, Vispain, speaking from outside my body saying, "you better take me back into you today or else." **The Devils were no longer in my body!**

I used to take 16 pills a day for different psychological conditions, had no job and was unemployable. Now, all this has changed. Thanks to Jesus working in this ministry.

Yes, I will always remember that day when Dr. Thomas R Snyder prayed for me and Jesus' resurrected power delivered me from a living hell of demons.

I give all the glory, honor and praise to Jesus.

This is how the children of light, under the power of the Holy Ghost, with boldness go into the enemy's camp, loosing those bound in darkness, through the power of God's love. Here was a man in his twenties, living in torment. Only the true power of God could deliver. This is the power that will deliver from the coming tribulation. It must be by the Holy Ghost. It's no wonder when Peter gave his first sermon after Pentecost, he said, *"Repent, and be baptized every one of you in the name of Jesus Christ for the remission of sins, and ye shall receive the gift of the Holy Ghost* (Acts 2:38). When the apostle Paul was passing through the coasts of Ephesus, he found certain disciples. It's interesting the first question he asked them is this, "Have ye received the Holy Ghost since ye believed?" *And they said unto him, We have not so much as heard whether there be any Holy Ghost* (Acts 19:2). These are truly exciting times we are living in. The scene is ready for a second pouring of the Holy Ghost. It's a good time to ask this question: "Have I received the gift of the Holy Ghost since I believed?" All you need to do is ask God in Jesus' name, and **he will send you the gift of the Holy Ghost !** *I (John) indeed baptize you with water unto repentance: but he that cometh after me is mightier than I, whose shoes I am not worthy to bear: he shall baptize you with the Holy Ghost, and with fire* (Matthew 3:11). *Jesus said, But the Comforter, which is the Holy Ghost, whom the Father will send in my name, he shall teach you all things, and bring all things to your remembrance, whatsoever I have said unto you* (John 14:26). God gives not as the world gives. Receiving the Holy Ghost in you is the key; you will not be left behind.

Many a prophet, in the word of God, has spoken of the days we are in. The Master, Jesus himself, spoke of these tribulation times. In order not to overfill our plate, the apostle John seems to be the best guide to navigate these waters. After all, wasn't it the apostle John who identified Satan at the Last Supper? *Simon Peter therefore beckoned to him, (John), that he should ask who it should be of whom he spake. He then lying on Jesus' breast saith unto him, Lord, who is it? Jesus answered, He it is, to whom I shall give a sop, when I have dipped it. And when he had dipped the sop, he gave it to Judas Iscariot, the son of Simon. And after the sop Satan entered into him. Then said Jesus unto him, That thou doest, do quickly* (John 13:24-27). The Apostle John is the only writer in the Bible that speaks of the antichrist. He also was the man God chose to write the book of Revelation. With this combination, we will clearly see the future.

Let's start the journey. *Little children, it is the last time: and as ye have heard that antichrist shall come, even now are there many antichrists; whereby we know that it is the last time* (1 John 2:18). *For many deceivers are entered into the world, who confess not that Jesus Christ is come in the flesh. This is a deceiver and an antichrist* (2 John: 7).

First we must understand the biblical definition of antichrist. Anyone who is "an opponent of the Messiah." What exactly does that mean? The Jewish people were waiting for the Messiah many years. Jesus came and filled the descriptive scriptures concerning the Messiah. However, they were blinded and denied the holy one of Israel, the Messiah. Although he came in the flesh, instead of receiving him, they became opponents to Jesus' God given position. Just as carnal Christianity, false religions, and devils persecute spiritual Christians today. *He came unto his own, and his own received him not. But as many as received him, to them gave he power to become the sons of God, even to them that believe on his name* (John 1:11-12). So when does the actual antichrist enter the world scene?

In the book of Revelation can be found where the devil will be forced out of the heavens down into another habitation, the earth. Not by his choice but by Almighty God's command. When Lucifer had his first habitation, in the presence of God, taken from him, his name was then changed to Satan. Then, when Jesus came to earth and Satan denied that he was the Messiah, his name was changed again to the devil. Once again, his habitation will be changed, when he no longer will be allowed to live in the heavens above the earth. His name will be changed to fit the status of his new habitation, to Dragon. *And I heard a loud voice saying in heaven, Now is come salvation, and strength, and the kingdom of God, and the power of his Christ: for the accuser of our brethren is cast down, which accused them before our God day and night. And they overcame him by the blood of the Lamb, and by the word of their testimony; and they loved not their lives unto the death. Therefore rejoice, ye heavens, and ye that dwell in them. Woe to the inhabiters of the earth and of the sea! for the devil is come down unto you, having great wrath, because he knoweth that he hath but a short time. And when the dragon saw that he was cast unto the earth, he persecuted the woman which brought forth the man child* (Revelation 12:10-13). As the devil is cast out of the heavens into his new habitation, the earth, his name is changed once again in midair to Dragon.

The name Dragon means: a fabulous kind of serpent; as supposed to fascinate. Once again, the scene is familiar, right back to the garden of Eden. The serpent now in possession of a new name 'Dragon.' In his true unchangeable character, he will seek to turn Eve's children against the word of God. But this time, the body of Christ, being the mobile tree of life, will reach out to the whole world, through the power of the Holy Ghost. To achieve this, there must be another Pentecost, latter rain, the pouring of the Spirit on all flesh!

Here again is the wisdom of God. Jesus had to leave his state of equality with God and take an existence in a fleshly body to redeem all of creation. Likewise, Satan will now take on or enter into another body, just like he did with Judas Iscariot. However, the difference this time is he cannot leave this habitation and go up into the heavens, leaving the body he was using behind. He is now a resident of the earth and has to contend with all the same conditions as you and I. God has removed all his escape routes. When he enters into another body, as he did with Judas Iscariot, **he now becomes the physical Antichrist.**

The Dragon then continues his defiance to Almighty God. Still wanting to exalt himself above the throne of God, he will need the cooperation of the human race to accomplish this feat. First thing he has to do is to raise himself up as a one world leader. This will take some time. He does this through trickery and lying signs and wonders. In the meanwhile, the true body of Christ will catch on fire through the pouring of the Holy Ghost. It will be the greatest day we have ever seen. Then, as the Dragon becomes more prominent, having a stranglehold on the world, he will issue a number, '666.' *And he causeth all, both small and great, rich and poor, free and bond, to receive a mark in their right hand, or in their foreheads: And that no man might buy or sell, save he that had the mark, or the name of the beast, or the number of his name. Here is wisdom. Let him that hath understanding count the number of the beast: for it is the number of a man; and his number is Six hundred threescore and six '666'* (Revelation 13:16-18). **DO NOT TAKE THIS NUMBER!** There is no more hope for anyone in possession of this number on their body. *And the third angel followed them, saying with a loud voice, If any man worship the beast and his image, and receive his mark in his forehead, or in his hand, The same shall drink of the wine of the wrath of God, which is poured out without mixture into the cup of his indignation; and he shall be tormented with fire and brimstone in the presence of the holy angels and in the presence of the Lamb* (Revelation 14:9-10). This scripture is a pre-requisite of the rapture and the tribulation.

The Dragon has been building himself up in power. This will take some time. Meanwhile, the church has been flourishing. Witnessing with power and the authority of the Holy Ghost, the truth about Jesus and the devil will be revealed to all that dwell on the face of the earth. Then the Dragon, who is Satan and the devil, makes it virtually impossible for the true believer to exist on earth without denying the faith by introducing the mark of the beast, "666." A good time for the rapture to take place?

Father God fully agrees. He sends Jesus in a cloud to receive his children. *And another angel came out of the temple, crying with a loud voice to him that sat on the cloud, Thrust in thy sickle and reap: for the time is come for thee to reap; for the harvest of the earth is ripe. And he that sat on the cloud thrust in his sickle on the earth, and the earth was reaped* (Revelation 14:15-16).

Now, you can clearly see why the rapture. You do not want to be left behind! The rapture's many facets will be thoroughly explored in the chapter titled 'Raptured! In the Twinkle of the Eye.' After the rapture has taken place, the scene on the earth will be drastically altered. Now instead of the Dragon persecuting the Saints, Almighty God begins to pour out his wrath on the Dragon and all the inhabitants of the earth. **THIS IS THE BEGINNING, THE GREAT TRIBULATION!** You may say this is unfair. How could a loving God do such a thing? Beloved, God has been patient and long-suffering with the human race. Time and time again, sending emissaries to represent the truth about creation. Many different tunes have been played, yet so many have gone to their own ways. Remember Methuselah, he was around all the business of God, yet wouldn't get his feet wet so to speak. The Bible was unfolding right before his very eyes. His father Enoch was raptured. His son Lamech's prophecy was being fulfilled. To put the icing on the cake, his grandson Noah was building an ark! Take a good look around, the scriptures are enfolding before the eyes of all mankind. Many people are only wanting peace and safety. Prosperity or increase is exactly what the Dragon will be offering all on the earth. To suffer for a little time only, seems to be one course never ordered on most plates. What will be in store for all that will be left on the earth?

We can find the tribulation's commencement in the sixteenth chapter of the book of Revelation. The rapture has already taken place in the fourteenth chapter of the same book. This is what is in store for those that are left behind:

* Verse two: noisome and grievous sores on all flesh.
* Verse three: every living soul dies in the sea.
* Verse four: all the rivers are turned to blood. This will become man's drinking water.
* Verse eight: the sun will give great heat, scorching man with fire.
* Verse ten: darkness that will cause man to gnaw their tongues in pain.
* Verse twelve: the great river Euphrates is dried up to prepare for a coming war—Armageddon.

Then not so surprising in verse fifteen, Jesus' mercies and compassion are seen once again. The reader is reminded of the rapture. He or she is reminded that they can escape all these horrible happenings that will come on the earth during the tribulation. *Behold, I come as a thief. Blessed is he that watcheth , and keepth his garments, lest he walk naked, and they see his shame* (Revelation 16:15).

* Verse seventeen: voices, and thunders, and lightnings; and a great earthquake, such as was not since man was upon the earth.
* Verse twenty one: hailstones one hundred pounds in weight. All this producing a society of blasphemers.

All verses referred to are from the sixteenth chapter of the book of Revelation.

There is only two ways to avoid entering into the tribulation; either a person dies by natural causes before the tribulation as Lamech did, or they must be raptured as Enoch was, the choice is yours!

What will happen when you leave this world and go into the next?

Exactly what will be the process of placement in heaven? What will the new world really be like? In our next chapter titled, 'The Books Were Opened,' a look through the windows of the scriptures awaits.

CHAPTER 11

The Books Were Opened

There isn't a person alive that hasn't looked up to the heavens, enveloped in their awesome existence, and not have had thoughts about eternity. Truly in the heart of man, there has been placed a desire to know what awaits them after leaving this earth. This is why when a miracle is witnessed or read about, it unlocks these areas of mysteries with divine reassurance. This divine reassurance confirms that there is a God, and he does communicate with man. As we look to the Bible, which is the inspired word of God, like a brush in an artist's hand, it will paint a perfect picture of clarity of what awaits us in heaven!

Two very distinct words seem to await the believer upon their arrival in Heaven. These words are *new* and *reward*. This will be the best day of their life! The books will be opened and all the business of this world will be finalized. *And I saw the dead, small and great, stand before God; and the books were opened: and another book was opened, which is the book of life: and the dead were judged out of those things which were written in the books, according to their works* (Revelation 20:12).

However, it will not go so well for the non-believer. This will be the worst possible day of their life. Why? Because this is exactly how judgment will take place. If your name is not written in the book of life, you go to hell! *And whosoever was not found written in the book of life was cast into the lake of fire* (Revelation 20:15). The only way to have your name recorded in this 'book of life' is by the blood of Jesus! It's not God's will for anyone to be excluded from this book; but through ignorance or rebellion, many a name will be excluded. **Don't be that person!** God extends his loving arms to everyone. *Who will have all men to be saved, and to come unto the knowledge of the truth. For there is one God, and one mediator between God and men, the man Christ Jesus* (1 Timothy 2:4-5).

The journey through this side of eternity will be completed. The books will be opened and Father God will first begin to make all things NEW, as only he can do. *And God shall wipe away all tears from their eyes; and there shall be no more death, neither sorrow, nor crying, neither shall there be any more pain: for the former things are passed away. And he that sat upon the throne said,* **"Behold, I make all things new."** *And he said unto me, Write: for these words are true and faithful* (Revelation 21:4-5). For all who have received Jesus as their Lord and Savior were born again and continued in the faith; despite the hardships of this world, their loving God and Father will personally place his hand on their face and comfort. Then, God will give to them a new body to live in; just like the Lord Jesus' resurrected body. Yes, a body that was able to enter into a room even when the doors are locked. A body that will have flesh and bones. A new body that will never wear out, experience pain or death. *Who shall change our vile body, that it may be fashioned like unto his glorious body, according to the working whereby he is able even to subdue all things unto himself* (Philippians 3:21).

Next, the Lord Jesus will give to everyone a new name. *He that hath an ear, let him hear what the Spirit saith unto the churches; To him that overcometh will I give to eat of that hidden manna, and will give him a white stone, and in the stone a new name written, which no man knoweth saving he that receiveth it* (Revelation 2:17). So many people love to name their children. They look at the character of the name or whom the name may remind them. Such thought is given to the naming of a child. Father God will exercise this same privilege with the naming of His eternal children.

Then, the Lord will replace this present earth and heavens, as we know them, with a new creation. Just like he did after the flood of Noah. However, the difference will be this new earth and new heavens will not have known sin. Father God and the Lord Jesus will dwell there in the celestial city with streets paved of gold. *And I saw a new heaven and a new earth: for the first heaven and the first earth were passed away; and there was no more sea. And I John saw the holy city, new Jerusalem, coming down from God out of heaven, prepared as a bride adorned for her husband* (Revelation 21:1-2).

This brings up the question, where will God place me in all of this? In turn, this brings us to the other books that will be opened on that day of judgment. Don't be deceived, the angels in heaven are recording every deed done in this earthly tabernacle. *For God shall bring every work into judgment, with every secret thing, whether it be good, or whether it be evil* (Ecclesiastes 12:14). Nehemiah writes, *Remember me, Oh my God, concerning this, and wipe not out my good deeds that I have done for the house of my God, and for the offices thereof* (Nehemiah 13:14). Yes, God remembers and has knowledge of everything you and I have ever done.

Here are two testimonies, in their own words, that will acknowledge that Father God is sovereign and omnipresent.

I have been smoking since the age of fifteen. That's ten years of smoking approximately two packs of cigarettes a day.

I have tried to quit smoking at least fifteen times, sometimes seriously, other times not. One time I even tried hypnotism-guaranteed to work!, but went right back smoking within days. Every time I tried to quit smoking, I was miserable, easily agitated, tense, on edge, and easily angered. For the past three years I have seriously tried to quit smoking, but was unsuccessful. The longest three weeks of total misery!

During the 'Evening of Miracles' meetings, I finally went to Dr. Thomas R Snyder and admitted that I could not quit smoking alone. I also have to admit my main purpose for prayer that evening was to see if God really could do such miracles. I was testing the Lord. I really had no desire to quit smoking. If I was going to quit, it was not my will but the Lord's!

The Lord spoke through Dr. Snyder, prophesying that for one week I would not be able to quit smoking. I would try but I would be miserable and unsuccessful. Then Jesus would fully deliver me. This would remove any doubt, it was the power of God. Without revealing my heart to Dr. Snyder, God knew my thoughts. It was true. It was a miserable week. Everything went wrong and there was no way I could quit smoking.

On Saturday morning of that week, I woke up and began smoking a cigarette. However, I did not know why I was smoking. It felt unnatural, even though that had been my morning routine for the past ten years. I put my cigarette out and haven't smoked since.

I have no desire to smoke, no withdrawal symptoms; I have not been tense or aggravated due to not smoking. Actually, being around others who smoke is undesirable and not tempting at all. I feel as though it has been ten to fifteen years since I had a cigarette.

Even through tribulation, the last thing on my mind is to have a cigarette. I have been 100% delivered from smoking. I give all glory to God. Praise the Lord!!!

Here is another testimony:

Why does God do things the way He does? We don't always understand, but we need to know His ways and His timing is perfect.

For four months, I suffered with an infection. I prayed and prayed, but nothing happened. I went to the doctor and bought some expensive medicine. When the medicine was gone, the infection was worse than before.

I sought out pastoral help and realized it was a spiritual problem, not a physical one. After being set straight in some areas, my faith was built up and I had a partial healing.

When I heard about the 'Evening of Mighty Miracles' with Dr. Thomas R Snyder, I knew in my heart I had to attend. My family also attended the meeting. At prayer time I went forward with my husband and Dr. Snyder asked us what we wanted Jesus to do for us. My husband and I asked for guidance in our lives and healing for my body. As Dr. Snyder laid hands on me, he spoke healing into my body in Jesus' matchless name. The power of God fell. And I was healed! I thank God for such a servant as Dr. Snyder. God is always faithful! I will continue to praise His holy name.

Pure and sure, Jesus knows every thought and deed we have ever performed. Not so much for condemnation but for reward. This is why we are advised by God's holy word to do all things in the name of Jesus. *And whatsoever ye do in word or deed, do all in the name of the Lord Jesus, giving thanks to God and the Father by him* (Colossians 3:17). This the world will not do, only the true believer. People that do not know Jesus are not aware of the heavenly bookkeeping. So wise they are, yet very foolish. Jesus advised Peter to have his mind and thoughts on heavenly things, not earthly. He also advises us if we think ourselves wise in this world, to make ourselves foolish. Not the type of fool that says in their heart that there is no God (Psalm 14:1), but the type of fool, in the world's eyes, that says there is a God!

Jesus, while on earth, revealed that in heaven there are many mansions. He also disclosed that he is preparing a place for the believer and one day will return in a cloud to receive all of God's children to himself; both dead and alive. This will be expounded on in the next chapter, titled 'Raptured! In the Twinkle of the Eye.' All who are counted worthy to attain to this first resurrection will not only occupy one of these mansions, but also sit at the Lord's table and dine with him.

There are three levels in heaven, just like there were three levels in Noah's ark. The apostle Paul was taken to the third level of heaven where God lives. *I knew a man in Christ above fourteen years ago, (whether in the body, I cannot tell; or whether out of the body, I cannot tell: God knoweth;) such an one caught up to the third heaven* (2 Corinthians 12:2). The Lord has designed a system of reward to place his children according to their deeds and works. In the bible, the book of Numbers in actuality also supports

Father God's rewarding character. *For the Son of man shall come in the glory of his Father with his angels; and then he shall reward every man according to his works* (Matthew 16:27). If the Lord did not want you or I to be aware of his rewarding character, he would not have included this revelation of his nature in so many scriptures.

Here are some scriptural examples of Father God's rewarding genius. *But without faith it is impossible to please him; for he that cometh to God must believe that he is, and that **he is a rewarder** of them that diligently seek him* (Hebrews 11:6). *Blessed are ye, when men shall revile you, and persecute you, and shall say all manner of evil against you falsely, for my sake. Rejoice, and be exceeding glad for <u>great is your reward in heaven:</u> for so persecuted they the prophets which were before you* (Matthew 5:11-12). Day after day God's true believers find themselves in many trials, as a result of living and doing the word of God (brokenness in their personal life along with the troubles in this dark and rebellious world). We are commanded to turn the other cheek. Suffer the wrong that the ministry be not blamed. Yes, lambs to the slaughter. **Cheer up, your reward will be great!**

An example of placement is given in a parable Jesus shared in the gospel of Luke. In the parable, a nobleman calls ten of his servants and gives each one a small sum of money. Then, tells them to represent him in his absence by using this money to their Lord's advantage. The society they lived in is described as one that hated the nobleman. The purpose of the nobleman's journey was to receive a kingdom not only for himself but also his loyal servants. Upon his return, the nobleman calls the ten servants to give an account of their deeds. The first one to appear before him tells him that the small sum of money gained his master tenfold. Here is the nobleman's answer. *Then came the first, saying, Lord, thy pound hath gained ten pounds. And he said unto him, Well, thou good servant: because thou hast been faithful in a very little, have thou authority over ten cities* (Luke 19:16-17). By Jesus speaking this parable, he reveals not only God's rewarding nature but gives us knowledge of what heaven will be like: cities, homes, governments, different levels of operation and honors. Jesus himself revealed to his twelve disciples, while on earth, that there will be two privileged children of God to sit one on his right hand and one on his left.

Jesus appears in heaven wearing many crowns. *His eyes were as a flame of fire and on his head were many crowns; and he had a name written, that no man knew but he himself. And he was clothed with a vesture dipped in blood: and his name is called The Word of God* (Revelation 19:12). This is how Jesus appears as the lion. A footnote, as was recorded earlier in this chapter, he that overcomes will receive a new name that would only be known to the person receiving the name. Here, even Jesus has received a name written that no man knows but himself. The word that was made flesh has now taken on a new demeanor. These crowns represent honor. All people will receive crowns on that day of judgment, a reflective of rewarding according to their deeds. Even the disobedient shall receive a crown.

The first crown given will be one of two, **a corruptible crown** or **an incorruptible crown**. *And every man that striveth for the mastery is temperate in all things. Now they do it to obtain a corruptible crown; but we an incorruptible crown* (1 Corinthians 9:25). This proves that God does love everyone and wills that he would have everyone saved, so much so that He also gives a crown to everyone who has chosen hell instead of heaven. These two crowns will also signify honor or dishonor. The believer receives an incorruptible crown; the non-believer receives a corruptible crown. Remember Ham, Noah's son, when he attained to the New World, he received a curse instead of a blessing.

Secondly, **a crown of rejoicing** can be had on that sweet and precious day of the Lord. *For what is our hope, or joy, or crown of rejoicing? Are not even ye in the presence of our Lord Jesus Christ at his coming* (1 Thessalonians

2:19). This crown of rejoicing will be given to all who heeded Jesus' words when he washed the disciples feet and said, "I am among you to serve." For the greatest of all is the servant of all.

Thirdly, **a crown of righteousness** will be given to all who love his appearing. *Henceforth there is laid up for me a crown of righteousness, which the Lord, the righteous judge, shall give me at that day: and not to me only, but unto all them also that love his appearing* (2 Timothy 4:8). When a person lives clean in mind, body, and soul, they are always before the Lord; desiring him to come quickly. You can tell such a person. Every day they desire not the things of this world but the things of God. Always filled with expectancy that this could be the day He will appear in the clouds to take them home.

Fourthly, **a crown of life** can be had by all who demonstrate their love for the Lord by enduring temptation. *Blessed is the man that endureth temptation: for when he is tried, he shall receive the crown of life, which the Lord hath promised to them that love him* (James 1:12). God has designed on this side of eternity, that everything you or I do will either receive a blessing or a curse. I am telling you these things because they are true. When the Israelites were traveling to the promise land, the Lord instructed Moses to place representatives from six tribes on one mountain and representatives from the other six tribes on another mountain. Moses then instructed the Levites to speak with a loud voice blessings and cursing. This was to be performed as the chosen people journeyed towards the promise land passing between these two mountains. This can be found in Deuteronomy 27: 11-14. Even as all mankind is traveling to the 'promised land,' which is heaven and judgment. With all of this said, all temptations are originated from two sources: the weakness of the flesh or the devil. God cannot tempt! When you or I are drawn away by our own lusts, sin lies at the door. The Lord knows the sacrifice one must make to endure temptation. So, Father God has designed a special crown for all who suffer such trials.

Fifthly, **a crown of glory** will be given to all elders, pastors, and so on who properly feed God's people being examples to the flock. Willingly doing service, by showing Christ's love to and through His people. *And when the chief Shepherd shall appear, ye shall receive a crown of glory that fadeth not away* (1 Peter 5:4).

So, why all these crowns? In the next world, the new heavens and new earth, these crowns are worn for honor or as in hell for dishonor. Besides the fashion statement they will make, honor or dishonor, they will also be used as worship expressions before the Lord. *The four and twenty elders fall down before him that sat on the throne, and worship him that liveth for ever and ever, and cast their crowns before the throne, saying, Thou art worthy, O Lord, to receive glory and honor and power: for thou hast created all things, and for thy pleasure they are and were created* (Revelation 4:10-11).

This is but a small glimpse of what awaits us in the next world heaven, paradise, the new Jerusalem and judgment. Nevertheless, to qualify for the rapture, seems to be the business at hand. In the next chapter titled, 'Raptured! In the Twinkle of the Eye,' the fog will lift; giving a clear understanding of God's essentials.

CHAPTER 12

Raptured!
In the Twinkle of the Eye

The great and mighty masterpiece of all is the glorious plan of rapture. Through this event, Father God makes an escape route for his people, while quarantining the devil, leaving him no escape route. Also bringing to light the reality that every believer must live by faith. Through the rapture, our Lord has devised a way to bring his banished home to himself without having to experience death or corruption. It is the only future event, in the heart of God, that can come at any time, as a thief in the night. Therefore, it is intended to keep one honest.

In previous chapters, much has been expounded concerning the different facets surrounding the rapture. This event is similar in some ways to the event of being "born again." Only because the carnal mind cannot apprehend it's reality, it can only be realized through revelation. The true believer not only will believe in it but will daily look for its appearing. The world on the other hand will laugh at any prospects of such an event. *Knowing this first, that there shall come in the last days scoffers, walking after their own lusts, And saying, Where is the promise of his coming? For since the fathers fell asleep, all things continue as they were from the beginning of the creation* (2 Peter 3:3-4). This is why it will come as a thief in the night on the whole earth.

While on earth, Jesus spoke a parable concerning this event. The parable can be found in the twenty-fifth chapter in the gospel of Luke. It speaks of the Lord of a household attending a wedding. In his absence, the servants are left to care for the daily business. They are instructed not only to be ready at their Lord's return, but that they were also required to serve. In verse forty of this parable can be found the prize we are looking for. *Be ye therefore ready also: for the Son of man cometh at an hour when ye think not* (Luke 12:40). A believer cannot afford to either be carnally minded or lukewarm. Both of these lifestyles will run the risk of being excluded in the rapture.

Leaving no stone unturned, this brings us to another parable. This parable will tie together the pouring of the Holy Ghost, latter rain, and the rapture. In the parable, which can be found in the twenty-fifth chapter of Matthew, there are ten virgins waiting for the bridegroom's coming. Five were wise having oil in their lamps, and five were foolish having no oil in their lamps. As they waited, it was business as usual. Surely, the five virgins not having oil in their lamps were aware of this condition. Sometimes when concerning the accomplishment of a desired purpose, it is easy to pretend, especially when hardships are involved. At midnight it was announced that the bridegroom is coming. The five virgins having no oil in their lamps trimmed them, and quickly realized they were empty. They make an attempt to acquire oil from the five virgins that were not foolish. They receive this disappointing answer; IT'S TOO LATE! So, they leave to acquire the missing ingredient. Meanwhile, the five wise virgins go into the wedding. When the five foolish virgins return, they find the door shut. To their amazement, missing the rapture, they are left behind! They learn this lesson too late: **God really means what he says.** *And while they went to buy, the bridegroom came; and they that were ready went in with him to the marriage: and the door was shut. Afterward came also the other virgins, saying, Lord, Lord, open to us. But he answered and said, verily I say unto you, I know* *you not. Watch therefore, for ye know neither the day nor the hour wherein the son of man cometh* (Matthew 25:10-13). Without exception, you must have the Holy Ghost in you! This is why, just like he did on Pentecost, God will pour out once again an abundant supply of fresh oil enough to fill all flesh. If necessary, there will be time to convert, as the apostle Peter had to, and be filled with this life changing force; or to continue just as you are. Once again, **THE CHOICE IS YOURS !**

When Jesus sent out his disciples, he sent them out two by two to the cities and towns that he would visit. *After these things the Lord appointed other seventy also, and sent them two and two before his face into every city and place, whither he himself would come* (Luke 10:1). These are not the original twelve disciples. At one point Jesus did send them (Matthew 10:5). Now, he was sending a larger number of representatives, as he will do in the latter rain. The Lord always sends his representatives out in twos. When Jesus was prophesying the end of times, he also shared this impeccable information. *I tell you, in that night there shall be two men in one bed; the one shall be taken, and the other shall be left. Two women shall be grinding together; the one shall be taken, and the other left. Two men shall be in the field; the one shall be taken, and the other left* (Luke 17:34-36). Just like in the parable of the ten virgins, those having the Holy Ghost in them will be taken; the others left. As it was shared earlier in the chapter titled, 'Boldness and Exploits,' both were involved with the Lord. Jesus cannot be served from the head, *only the heart!* What a day that will be! Can you imagine that? To meet the Lord Jesus in the air and be with him forever. Hallelujah!

No one has to be excluded from the rapture. Remember Methuselah? He watched and ignored all the signs around him. God is not about death or sorrows; he is about life.

Here is a testimony, in her own words, showing this unparallel nature of God.

Words cannot express the gratitude I have in my heart for you and this ministry. Not only has Jesus healed us of so many different sicknesses and pains, he has sustained our family for years.

Healing started with a level one cancer cells in my cervix, which I was told by doctors that my chances were very high for miscarriage, due to the surgery to remove the cells. When I was given another report, two years later, that the pre-cancer cells were returning, I came to Dr. Thomas R Snyder for prayer. Dr. Snyder, you prayed for me at a camp fire meeting, and Jesus healed me of the cancer that threatened not only my life, but my hearts desire to be a mother.

I thank Jesus for his great mercies and healing! I have given birth to four beautiful children and I am still cancer free.

Many are confused about the last trump and the end of the world. They are mixing the two together. When the last trump sounds, this will not be the end of time. The world will still exist, awaiting the tribulation that shall come upon all the earth.

In order to clarify this, the apostle Paul in his last letter enlightens us to the fact that when the first resurrection takes place, the earth will still remain. *Who concerning the truth have erred, saying that the resurrection is past already; and overthrow the faith of some* (2 Timothy 2:18). The early believers had knowledge that there would be a first resurrection from the dead; not only of the Saints that are deceased, but also all that are still alive at the time. If this first resurrection meant that it was the end of the world, how could they spread rumors that it has already taken place? There would be no world! Therefore, logic dictates that the world will remain after the rapture.

With this revelation, we can now clearly understand exactly how the rapture will take place, leaving the world intact. *In a moment, in the twinkling of an eye, at the last trump: for the trumpet shall sound, and the dead shall be raised incorruptible, and we shall be changed* (1 Corinthians 15:52). The confusion here comes from these words "the dead shall be raised." One might think this to infer all who have died. On the contrary, a further search of the scriptures will produce the antidote. *But the rest of the dead lived not again until the thousand years were finished. This is the first resurrection* (Revelation 20:5). Only the dead in Christ or anyone who died as a believer will be raised at this point in time. *For the Lord himself shall descend from heaven with a shout, with the voice of the archangel, and with the trump of God: and the dead in Christ shall rise first: Then we which are alive and remain shall be caught up together with them in the clouds, to meet the Lord in the air: and so shall we ever be with the Lord* (1 Thessalonians 4:16-17). **This is the rapture!**

The apostle John was in the spirit on the Lord's day when he was called up into heaven with a trump. *After this I looked, and, behold, a door was opened in heaven: and the first voice which I heard was as it were of a trumpet talking with me; which said, Come up hither, and I will shew thee things which must be hereafter. And immediately I was in the spirit; and, behold, a throne was set in heaven and one sat on the throne* (Revelation 4:1-2). The Holy Ghost is essential to anyone attaining to the rapture. First, you must be born again. *Marvel not that I say unto the, Ye must be born again* (John 3:7). If you have not received a born again experience, invite Jesus into your heart today. Repent and make your peace with God. Then Peter said unto them *"Repent, and be baptized every one of you in the name of Jesus Christ for the remission of sins, and ye shall receive the gift of the Holy Ghost"* (Acts 2:38). If you have been baptized into the faith by water and have not received the Holy Spirit, you only need to ask in Jesus' name. God will fill you with the Holy Ghost. *If ye then, being evil, know how to give good gifts unto your children: how much more shall your heavenly Father give the Holy Spirit to them that ask him?* (Luke 11:13)

What we are experiencing today, the wars, earthquakes, pestilences, false prophets, and other troubles are the beginning of sorrows. This is not the end of the world or the final tribulation. See Matthew 24:8,11.

Here is an outline of the course of events:*

1) The pouring out of the Holy Spirit.-Revelation 10:11
2) The two witnesses.-Revelation 11:3
3) The casting out of the devil unto the earth.-Revelation 12:9
4) The devil sits in the temple proclaiming himself God. 2 Thessalonians 2: 4, Revelation 13:6
5) The number 666 is given.-Revelation 13:16-18
6) The rapture.-Revelation 14:15
7) The great tribulation.-Revelation 16:1
8) The devil is bound for 1000 years.-Revelation 20:2
9) The thousand year reign of Jesus Christ on earth.-Revelation 20:6
10) The great battle, Gog and Magog.-Revelation 20:8
11) The devil (Satan, the serpent, the Dragon, Lucifer) cast into hell.-Revelation 20:10
12) The judgment.-Revelation 20:12
13) The new heavens and a new earth.-Revelation 21:1

In my closing, I would like to share a visitation I received some 30 years ago. The apostle Paul, on the road to Damascus was met with none other than Jesus Christ himself. He appeared to him as a light from heaven (Acts 9:3).

*   This is only a glimpse of a very detailed future of events.

I had been a born-again believer for not very long, about two or three years. Being very zealous for the work of God, I had filled my house with some challenging guests. They were spending the night, for different reasons, nevertheless, they were there. One guest was an ex-Hells Angel, a rather large man with his lady in tow and three small children. His body guard chose to stay outside and sleep in their automobile. Also staying for the weekend was my cousin, whom I had been witnessing to about the love of Jesus. She was an inmate at a correctional institution nicknamed 'Hells Kitchen' in New York City. I was able to receive her out for the weekend. The scene was set. Things began to unravel. My houseguests only wanted to talk about their experiences from the dark side of life. All my efforts to witness seem to fail. I kept thinking what a mistake I made. Perhaps, I let my emotions move me instead of my Lord. I went to bed brokenhearted, as they stayed up reminiscing of old times.

As I lay there in my bed unable to sleep, with tears in my eyes, still brokenhearted, a most divine happening suddenly appeared. It was around three or four in the morning, a shaft of light about eighteen inches round entered in through the outside wall of my home. I had never felt such peace like this before in my life, nor have I ever since. What beauty! What peace! As this light moved across the room towards an inside wall, the room stayed dark in front of it. However, immediately behind the darkness, it was light, a light such as I have never seen in my whole life. The eighteen inch round shaft of light was one color and the haze or Shekinah glory around it was another kind of light. **My eyes were fully opened!** I was then asked a question in my mind. "What are you feeling?" My reply was, "I am feeling such peace. There is nothing that could disturb me, bother me, or hurt me in any way. No matter what happened to me, nothing could affect me or take me out of this peace." Also I might add, that it was controlling me and I could only speak truth. No lies, none of my own thoughts, just enveloped in intoxicating peace. I later learned that this was an extension of the Lord Jesus from His throne.

I've carried this heavenly vision with me for many years, and it is still as fresh to me today as the day I witnessed it. You might be wondering what happened to the houseguests. The rather large fellow woke up crying and crying and crying. He asked me if I had a Bible that he could have. I told him it's not so much the Bible you want, it's salvation for your soul. With tears flowing down from both of our eyes, he received both the Bible and Jesus as his Lord and Savior. He then contacted the authorities concerning some criminal deeds he had committed and was placed in prison for a short time. My female cousin felt a burning inside her belly exactly at the time when the shaft of light entered. When I awoke in the morning, she was gone. Returning a few weeks later, she explained what happened, telling me then about the burning in her belly. After a brief sharing, she also accepted Jesus as her Lord and Savior. The female companion of the ex-Hells Angel was healed of cancer.

Jesus is the same yesterday, today and forever. He belongs to the whole human race. You only have to want him. There is not one person on this earth today that has to be excluded in the rapture and go through the tribulation. **THE CHOICE IS YOURS!**

Contacts

To contact the author write:

P.O Box 7299

Brandon, Fl. 33508

or

Dr. Thomas R Snyder

Senior Pastor

Lamb of God Christian Center

5707 31st Avenue South

Tampa, FL 33619

www.LambofGodctn.org

christianctr@verizon.net